CONCILIUM

Religion in the Seventies

CONCILIUM

TRUTH AND CERTAINTY

Edited by
Edward Schillebeeckx and
Bas van Iersel

Herder and Herder

1973
HERDER AND HERDER NEW YORK
815 Second Avenue
New York 10017

ISBN: 0–8164–2539–6

Cum approbatione Ecclesiastica

Library of Congress Catalog Card Number: 72–12421

Printed in the United States

CONTENTS

Editorial 7

PART I

ARTICLES

I. HISTORICAL DEVELOPMENT OF THE
PROBLEM

Norms of Christian Allegiance and Identity in the
History of the Church 11
YVES CONGAR

Truth and Verification at Vatican I 27
GUSTAVE THILS

Aspects of the Truth in the New Testament 35
JEAN GIBLET

The Person and Office of Peter in the New Testament 42
JOSEF BLANK

II. INTERDISCIPLINARY CONSIDERATIONS

Certainty, Truth and the Church's Teaching Office 56
IRING FETSCHER

The Concept of Infallibility 65
PATRICK MCGRATH

III. THE PROBLEM OF THE INFALLIBILITY
OF THE CHURCH'S OFFICE

A Theological Reflection 77
EDWARD SCHILLEBEECKX

IV. PETER AS THE FOUNDATION STONE IN THE
     PRESENT UNCERTAINTY   95
RENE LAURENTIN

PART II

DOCUMENTATION

A Hundred Years after Vatican I: Some Light on the
Concept of Infallibility   117
ANTON HOUTEPEN

A Short Balance-Sheet of the Debate on Infallibility   129
HANS KUNG

Biographical Notes   137

Editorial

"TRUTH" is the key-word in this number of *Concilium* and it forms the basis of a discussion about the Roman Catholic view concerning the lasting character of the Church and the "charism of truth" that God has promised to the "unity of the Church's office", a charism which, according to the First Vatican Council, results in certain cases in "infallible judgment about faith".

Our primary intention is not to consider critically certain recent publications such as the Castelli symposium, *L'infaillibilité. Son aspect philosophique et théologique* (Paris, 1970) or Hans Küng's book, *Infallible? An Enquiry* (London, 1972) and the controversy that has raged around it. All the same, it is hardly possible to avoid theological reflection about the difficulties raised in such works.

Since one of the two editors responsible for this number has himself written a synthetic concluding article, there is no need for this editorial to be very long. In the first place, the historical development of the whole problem is discussed in a group of four articles. Yves Congar's data from the history of the Church are contrasted with the First Vatican Council's concept of truth (G. Thils). In turn, this conciliar concept is confronted with data from the New Testament (J. Giblet and J. Blank).

This group of articles is followed by an interdisciplinary approach, in which a sociologist, Iring Fetscher, uses a sociological model to interpret and assess the Roman Catholic affirmation of infallibility, which he treats, of course, as a sociological datum. Patrick McGrath criticizes the dogma from the point of view of

7

linguistic analysis.

Finally, in a synthetic article, questions are asked, firstly, about the context in which the "dogma of infallibility" ought to function, if it is to be meaningful, and, secondly, about the real ecclesiological significance of "infallibility" (E. Schillebeeckx).

It is well known how much alarm can be caused among the ordinary members of the Church if they are left without pastoral guidance when a dogma is reformulated, however faithful this new formulation may be to the Gospel. René Laurentin therefore supplements the historical and theological reflections in this number by a pastorally orientated article.

The last two contributions form a bibliographical documentation based on recent publications about the dogma of Vatican I. These have been written by Anton Houtepen and, because he has played a leading part in the recent controversy, Hans Küng.

EDWARD SCHILLEBEECKX
BAS VAN IERSEL

PART I
ARTICLES

I. Historical Development of the Problem

Norms of Christian Allegiance and Identity in the History of the Church[1]

Yves Congar

THE Church, the people of God under the messianic order, is an *established* religious reality deriving from gifts of revelation and life made by God in a series of historic and therefore unique interventions which found their consummation in the coming of Jesus Christ and the sending of the Holy Spirit. The unity of the Church is bound up with the uniqueness of the moment and aspect which instituted and constituted that same origin (cf. Mt. 16. 16). Its entire history and expansion pose the question of its identity through allegiance to that origin—a chain of allegiance whose first link and guarantee are the Twelve and Paul.

From the Apostolic Age, there is a fundamental reference to identity and allegiance in the profession of faith that "Jesus Christ is Lord" (cf. Rom. 10. 9; Ph. 2. 11; 1 Cor. 12. 3; Acts 17. 7), which, in Paul's preaching, turns into an anathematizing of anyone who tries to announce "another gospel": other, that is, than the gospel of justification by faith in the "Lord Jesus Christ, who ... gave himself for our sins" (Gal. 1. 3–9). In the congregations there is not only the rule of homophony (Clement, *Cor.* 51. 2; cf. 1 Cor. 1. 10) but a discipline in terms of traditions which have to be respected (1 Cor. 11. 2), or in regard to moral behaviour, to which a sanction may be applied in the form of excommunication (cf. 1 Cor. 5. 1–5; Mt. 18. 15–18; Tit. 3. 10).

[1] Since the present article is an historical survey, footnotes are requisite. In order to avoid loading the pages too much below, I give at the end of the article a list of works to which I refer by means of a letter followed by a page number reference.

I. From Clement of Rome to Cyprian

The principle or norm of allegiance, or faithfulness, is the "rule of truth" or "rule of faith".[2] This is not a formal norm in regard to faith itself, but the very substance of that faith: *that which* the apostles handed down, having received it from Jesus Christ, and the Church has handed down after them, in so far as it is normative for belief (for tradition also transmits cultic rules, disciplinary elements in regard to which legitimate differences may exist between Churches). It is not a matter of "infallibility"; but this "rule" deriving from the apostles, the apostles of Christ and the Christ of God,[3] was taken as and was henceforth to be taken as quite assuredly mediating the absolute truth.[4]

It is what the Church preaches and believes. It has a transcendental guarantee: God himself, who is the origin; Christ who embodied it and who is *the* Truth; and the Spirit, of whom Irenaeus says he is the *communicatio Christi* and also *the* Truth.[5] But this announcement of truth has an historical reality. Its assurance of truth is that of the historical mediations by means of which the absolute truth of God is communicated to us. Essentially there is only one mediation: that of the Church, which is also divine in origin. The way of being in the truth is to live in the communion, or community, of the Church. The faith of the Church is assured of accordance with the faith of the apostles by virtue of (*a*) its conformity to what was handed down by the primitive authors, who had themselves received it, and thus back to the very start;[6] (*b*) the succession of presbyters or episcopes who teach in the Church;[7] (*c*) recourse to the Scriptures, which

---

[2] Cf. G, vol. I, pp. 44 f., which supplies the references to the authors and to C. Add: B. Häggelund, "Die Bedeutung der 'regula fidei' als Grundlage theologischer Aussage", in *Studia theologica*, 12 (1958), pp. 1–44.

[3] Tertullian, *Praescr.* 37, 1; Clement, *Cor.* 42.

[4] Cf. Irenaeus, *A.H.* III, 5, 1; 12, 6; V, 33, 7 and 8; V, praef. and 20; Tertullian, *Praescr.* 28 and 29.

[5] Christ. truth: Irenaeus, *A.H.*, III, 5, 1; Tertullian, *De virg. vel.*, 1; Cyprian, Epist. 74. 9 (=Jn. 14. 6). Spirit: *A.H.* III, 24, 1.

[6] Cf., e.g.: Polycarp, *Philip.* 7, 1–2 (up to 110).

[7] Cf., *inter al.*: Irenaeus, *A.H.* III, 2. 2 and 3. 2; IV, 26. 2 and 4; Origen, *De Princ.* I, proem., 2; *In Mat. com. ser.* 46. Apart from C and I, see A. Ehrhardt, *The Apostolic Succession in the First Two Centuries of the Church* (London, 1953), pp. 107–31.

contain all wholesome truth (cf. G, vol. I, pp. 139 f.). Until the
middle of the second century, "Scriptures" generally referred to
the Old Testament, the *paradosis* of which was interpretation in
the sense of the "mystery" of Christ. Then the New Testament
was joined to the Old; its canon was fixed in the second century
in accordance with the criterion of apostolical provenance (see
R). Yet there is no heresy that does not invoke Scripture, which
does not have recourse to it for fragments which are then turned
to different ends. Scripture ought to be read *in the Church*, where
"the apostles deposited the perfect fullness of truth", under the
aegis of the presbyters "apud quos est apostolica doctrina".[8]

Are the episcopes (presbyters) criteria of truth or of allegiance
(faithfulness)? And, if so, on what ground? History shows that
many heresies and schisms originated from or were espoused by
bishops. Irenaeus, even though he acknowledges the hypothesis,
speaks of "charisma veritatis certum", a phrase whose interpretation is disputed.[9] The idea of a gift of the Spirit in those who
are to assure the faithfulness of the *paradosis* is well-attested,
without any mechanistic help from an authority invested in an
institution by Christ, but in the following sense: it is the Spirit
who guarantees belief in Jesus Christ (1 Cor. 12. 3; 1 Jn. 4. 2–3
and 5. 6), the *communicatio Christi* (cf. n. 5), the faithful transmission of the deposit of faith (cf. 2 Tim. 1. 14), the authenticity
and the value of ministries,[10] and, in fact, the effectiveness of the
admonitions and interventions of ordained ministers.[11]

There is a handed-down *paradosis* of the Holy Spirit which,
for Hippolytus, would seem to be invested in the "diadoques"
of the apostles by virtue of ordination.[12] Even though a bishop
may err, the unanimity of the episcopate, like that of Churches,

[8] Irenaeus, *A.H.* III, 4. 1; IV, 26. 5 and 32. 1; V, 20. 1; Origen, *In Mat.
com. ser.* 46, etc.

[9] *A.H.* IV, 26. 2. Two interpretations: (1) objective meaning, the doctrine
of the Church (K. Müller; C, pp. 186–7; E. Molland; D, p. 188; R. P. C.
Hanson; preference of A. Benoit). (2) Charism of office (Gregory Dix;
N. Brox; W. Telfer; L. Ligier; I, pp. 203–7).

[10] Cf. Acts 1. 2; 20. 28; Clement, *Cor.* 42. 4; Hippolytus, *Trad. apost.*,
3 (prayer of consecration of a bishop).

[11] Cf. Acts 15. 28, where Harnack sees some support for a concept of infallibility; Clement, *Cor.* 8. 1; 42. 3; 63. 2.

[12] Cf. *Philosophoumena* I, *praef.* 6 (G, vol. I, pp. 52 and 102 n. 62).

is a good criterion of truth (above all Cyprian: cf. C, pp. 239 ff.; 245; G, vol. I, p. 102, n. 61; and particularly, O).

Among the Churches, has the Church of Rome, and among the bishops, has the bishop who occupies the *cathedra Petri*, a special charism of truth and a superior authority? Whatever position one may adopt in regard to the meaning of two texts which are as discussed as they are famous, Irenaeus, *A.H.* III, 3. 2 and Cyprian, *De unitate*, c. 4 and 5, long version (challenged by O, who attributes it to Optatus), one cannot deny the Roman Church of the second and third centuries a role of *vinculum unitatis*. To talk of a "*criterion* of communion" would perhaps be an exaggeration, but it is permissible to talk of a centre and reference for communion.[13] The possible legal implications of this fact are still not elucidated as such. The role of bishops is not to impose *their* authority but to refer to tradition; to exhort the deviant to conform to tradition, and to persuade them by means of Scripture (cf. D).

II. The Fathers of the Classic Epoch and the High Middle Ages

As in the preceding age, the standard of allegiance and of identity is the faith of the Church, and therefore tradition in the most comprehensive sense. Two features are especially characteristic of a new situation: (1) this faith of the Church is henceforth considered as formulated in texts: Scripture, Councils, "Fathers". (2) As the Church spreads and new and very serious heresies arise, and the Churches organize their liturgical and canonical life, the function of reference and preservation is insufficient: that of creativity and decision has to be exercised (the theme of M). The most decisive instance in this respect was, in the ninth century, the introduction of the *filioque* into the liturgical profession of faith in the Frankish Church, in spite of Pope Leo III. In the thirteenth century this addition—or explanation—was attributed to the authority of the Roman Church.

[13] Cf. J. F. McCue, "The Roman Primacy in the Second Century and the Problem of Development of Dogma", *Theol. Studies* 26 (1964), pp. 161–96; G. D'Ercole, "Communio interecclesiastica e valutazione giuridica del primato del vescovo di Roma nelle testimonianze patristiche dei primi tre secoli", *Apollinaris* 35 (1962), pp. 25–75.

The infallibility is that of God. It extends to the Scriptures, which contain all wisdom requisite for salvation, *veritas secundum pietatem* (Tit. I. I): it is the absolute reference (G, vol. I, pp. 142–3). One has only to search Scripture to elucidate its meaning. The profession of faith refers to Scripture and to tradition handed down since the apostles.[14] Nevertheless, the Church had to define its creed in the Councils, in face of heresies. From what source do these Councils derive their authority: various answers are given. From the perfect conformity of their definitions to Scripture and tradition as received since the apostles: Athanasius and others after him (P, 1970; 1971, pp. 63–5 and 385). According to Nicaea, from the charismatic nature of the Fathers, confessors and martyrs (P, 1971, p. 58). From the assistance of the Holy Spirit and the presence of Christ who presides over them in mystical form (P, 1970, p. 386 [Constantine] and 1971, pp. 59–61). From the unanimity of the Fathers representing that of the Churches: unanimity being laid down in classical philosophy, and even more firmly in Christianity, as the mark of the action of the Spirit (cf. P, 1971, pp. 65 and 364–86 on Vincent of Lérins); "Securus judicat orbis terrarum" (Augustine, *C. epist. Parmen.* III, 4; 24). From the presence of representatives of the Bishop of Rome, says Pope Damasus (P, 1971, p. 68). Sometimes, the *written* definition of the Councils is given the character and value of an *auctoritas ecclesiastica* (Vincent: P, 1971, pp. 373 ff.). The Councils express the faith of the Church: it is known through the consensus apparent in them, and through that which is accorded them in the process of their acceptance (cf. J).

Is an authority of the "magisterium" (to use a word of relatively recent date in this particular acceptation) accorded to the *praepositi Ecclesiae* (here it is the contemporary usage)? A juridical authority cannot be separated from that which derives from spiritual charisms: the Councils and the "Fathers" are inspired, *theopneustoi*.[15] Interesting and noteworthy in this respect is the

[14] Cf. the beginning of the profession of faith proposed at Nicaea by Eusebius of Caesarea (Hahn, *Bibl. d. Symbole*, p. 257); Athanasius himself on Nicaea (P, art. of 1970); Gregory of Nyssa, *Contra Eunomium*, c. 4 (PG 45, 653); etc.

[15] Cf. G. vol. I, pp. 151–8; A. Lauras, "S. Léon le Grand et la Tradition", *Rech. Science Relig.* 48 (1960), pp. 166–84 (pp. 175 *et seq.*).

use of the words *aplanès, aplanètos*, which mean: fixed, that which does not deviate, unerring, sure. I have read the texts cited by G. W. H. Lampe. Their connotations are more spiritual than juridical. However, the bishops, in council, claim to be able to define *hôrizeïn*, definitively and, in matters of faith, irrevocably: cf., for example, the famous canon 7 of the Council of Ephesus, 431. They subscribe to the canons or the dogmatic *horoi* with the formula, "*horisas*, definiens subscripsi". Justinian I said that he considered the teachings of the first four general Councils to be the word of God, and their canons to be laws of the Empire (Nov. 131, c. 1: cf. Basilicorum lib. V, tit. III, c. 2). It is known that St Gregory the Great put the first four Councils on the same level as the four gospels. As for the Byzantine Emperors, they more than once tried to re-create or to impose a unity of belief on their subjects by means of certain rather unfortunate decrees (cf. E 151 ff.).

In regard to the Roman Church and its bishop, we must first of all remember one very important point: the latter is never separated from the former. A second point is that the understanding of the role of Rome as the centre and criterion of communion in the faith is not the same in Rome, and in the West, as in the East. Of course, in a broad sense, this understanding to some degree exists everywhere.[16] In Rome there was the conviction, shared later by the West, that Peter was still living there: a pope did not succeed his predecessor, but Peter. After Damasus (366–84) there arose the idea according to which Rome, as the head or the source, incorporates in a unique and superior way all the titles of the Church: the apostolicity and apostolic traditions (Innocent I, 401–17: M, pp. 81–2), catholicity,[17] the privilege which the spiritual man enjoys of judging everything, or of not being judged by anyone (a juridical transposition, and then an application to the *prima sedes* of the spiritual anthropology of

[16] The studies of L. Hertling ("Communio und Primat", *Miscellanea Hist. Pontificae* VII, 1943, pp. 1–48) and of G. D'Ercole would require a critical analysis in order to apprehend full value. See also J. Lecuyer, "La communion épiscopale dans les conciles africains entre 400 et 425: Au service de la parole de Dieu", *Mélanges Mgr. Charue* (Gembloux, 1969), pp. 101–22.

[17] The Roman Church = *universalis* (M 156); Nicholas I sees it as an epitome of the whole Church.

1 Cor. 2. 15: cf. B, pp. 297 f.). It is to the Roman Church or to the apostolic See that it is necessary not only to conform in matters of discipline or custom, but to refer "quoties fidei ratio ventilatur".[18] In fact, "in sede apostolica immaculata est semper catholica servata religio", proclaims Hormisdas, in the formulation given to the Eastern bishops after the schism of Acacia in August 515. Note in this formula the word *servata*, which takes all its force from the word before it: "Prima salus est regulam sanctae fidei custodire et a constitutis patrum nullatenus deviare" (DSch. 363).

The West accepted this theology: not without some resistance (ninth and tenth centuries) to an excessively monarchical ideology, but in the deep religious belief that there was no Church without communion with the See of Peter. In Africa Optatus of Milevis developed the Roman conception. Even the Augustinian exegesis of Mt. 16. 16 ff., "uni, quia unitati", ended up by being taken in the Roman sense, for the Pope appeared as the representation of the whole Church and was therefore seen as incorporating its charisms. The East, on the other hand, whereas it allowed Rome the canonical privileges of the *prima sedes*, did not accept the value *ex sese* of the decisions of this See and held to the synodal structure of supreme courts of appeal: not, unfortunately, without frequent concessions to imperial pretensions which tended to counter the principle of apostolicity (see the work of A. Michel and N, pp. 100 ff.).

III. FROM THE GREGORIAN REFORM TO THE SIXTEENTH CENTURY

This era was decisive: canonical scholarship and scholastic theology formed the concepts, vocabulary and structures, which, reinforced by the Counter-Reformation and the nineteenth-century Restoration, remained dominant until Vatican II. The break (almost complete) with the Byzantine East, and then the Slavic East, gave complete freedom for deployment of the analytical and legal genius of the West: all the more since the necessary battle against the domination of secular powers, then later against rationalist dissociations, demanded from the Church a concen-

---

[18] Innocent I, 27. 1. 417: PL 20, 590. Reproduced by Gratian (C 12, C XXIV, q. 1), this text was, in the thirteenth century, to ground the idea that it was the responsibility of the pope to determine the *articuli fidei*.

tration on its bases, and on its institutional foundation; the Church found security and strength in the Law and in the support of the Roman rock—*super petram.*

One should not underestimate, in this respect, the importance of the reformation which began with Leo IX, Nicholas II and Gregory VII, and which required the creation of new canonical collections, and then of a new canonical science—the fruit of which was the Decree of Gratian (1140), a kind of "Denzinger" of the Middle Ages (though less selective than Denzinger).[19] The Gregorian Church emerged from its dovetailing with the Empire; it was given an independence of Law and hierarchical structures, finding its support in the apostolic authority of the Roman Pontiff. The latter claimed the right to change canons, whereas the emperor's supporters wanted to maintain the *status quo* (cf. M, pp. 265 ff., 274–8, 292 f.). The pope, together with the cardinals, *pars corporis papae*, whose authority increased and whose consistory tended to replace the former Roman synods, appeared as the sovereign legislature. A Catholic obeyed its authority and conformed to the Roman Church. A heretic opposed it.[20] Such was the new form taken by the ancient and traditional, which turned the faith of the *Ecclesia* into a rule of catholicity or orthodoxy. Therefore the idea prevailed that the rule of faith was the *paradosis* of the Church; yet the idea of "tradition" tended to concentrate on the norm of the Roman Church, which was itself founded on Scripture (Mt. 16. 18: "Quodcumque ligaveris . . ."). It was always the will of God which was the absolute norm, and constantly proclaimed as such. But this will was known in terms of its essential centre: the sacerdotal-papal centre. Whereas the life of the Church was regulated by conciliar canons or maxims deriving from the Fathers (cf. F), there was a movement after Gratian and with the canonist-popes who, after Alexander III, were to be the most numerous, to a law of pontifical "Gesetzgebung" (the conciliar decisions were presented as *papal* decisions: cf. N, pp. 151 ff.).

This entire process may be characterized as a process of juridi-

---

[19] See my *L'Ecclésiologie du haut moyen âge* (Paris, 1968).

[20] The text preferred by Gregory VII is 1 S 15, pp. 22–3. *Dictatus papae* XXVI (in 1075): "Quod catholicus non habeatur qui non concordat Romanae Ecclesiae" (ed. Caspar, Reg. II 55a; comp, VII, 24, with notes p. 207 and p. 504).

cization of ecclesiological values which, at the start, derived from a more moral and charismatic spiritual context. Examples are Jer. 1. 10 and 1 Cor. 2. 15; 6. 3, which become the right to depose kings; similarly Rev. 19, 16, *rex regum*, a christological and eschatological text, was transferred to the pope, the "vicar of Christ", and so on.

The more doctrinal activity of the See of Rome remained quite restricted; it operated against errors (Béranger of Tours, Abelard, and then later the dualist or anti-ecclesiastical heresies). The most prominent event in this regard was the intervention in 1177 of Alexander III against the "christological nihilism" attributed to Peter Lombard (DSch. 749, 750; cf. N, p. 191). Even when Gratian (who certainly did not minimize papal authority) attributed to the pope primacy in the *juridical* domain, and the primacy in the interpretation of Scripture to Holy Doctors, "sicut pleniori gratia Spiritus sancti, ita ampliori scientia aliis precellentes" (*dictum ante*, c. 1 D. XX), the commentators on the *Decree*, and above all the theologians of the thirteenth century, subordinated the teaching of the Doctors and even of the Fathers to the authority of the Roman Pontiff.[21] Here we are at the start of the process which led to the dogma of 18 July 1870. But we are not there yet. Everyone held then that immunity from error was proper to the *Ecclesia* itself (relying above all on the substantiation of the text of Lk. 22. 32); and that the pope and any member of the Roman Church could err (cf. N, pp. 244 ff.).

Within the overall framework of an unusual growth in the role of the papacy, three factors were involved in the attribution to the pope of a doctrine of infallibility: (1) the principle formulated by Innocent I, often resorted to thereafter (in particular by the pseudo-Isidore whose texts are also reproduced by Gratian [c. XXIV q. 1]) that the "Roman Church has never erred in belief". But the following general interpretation was given: the Roman Church = the universal Church (N, p. 245); (2) the idea of "representation": a concept firmly inscribed in the Catholic understanding of ecclesiology,[22] and active throughout its history,

[21] See Thomas Aquinas, II^a-II^æ, 10, 12; *Quodl.* IX, 16; F 188 ff.; N. p. 298.

[22] Cf. C. Schmitt, *Römischer Katholizismus und politishe Form* (Munich, 1925), pp. 26–53.

though more active in the framework of the corporative notions of the twelfth and thirteenth centuries, and in that of Aristotle's *Politics*. The head, *caput*, of a community, incorporates and, in this organic sense, represents the entire community. The Doctors of the thirteenth century moved in this way from the *Ecclesia* to the pope (N 246), as did Gui Terré in the fourteenth century (S 244–6). (3) The Franciscan debate on absolute poverty caused a decisive importance to be attributed, first of all to the canonization of St Francis (which posed the question of the infallibility of the pope in canonizations),[23] then to the defence (by Olivi) of the irrevocability of a papal judgment; in fact, Nicholas III had proclaimed that the way of St Francis was the very one followed by Christ and the apostles (*Exiit*, August 1279); his successor, John XXII, could give no other judgment, Olivi maintained, since a pope's judgment is irrevocable and exempt from error. Brian Tierney has shown (S) that the first affirmation of the *infallible* character of a papal doctrinal judgment was made upon the basis of these suggestions of Olivi's. It was in this debate started by Olivi that the Carmelite Gui Terré, who defended John XXII, maintained, shortly before 1328 (for the first time in so formal a manner) that the pope "apud quem residet auctoritas ecclesie catholice" cannot err when he defines an article of faith (H 110 ff., S 238 ff.).

This did not imply a suppression of the infallibility of the Church as such, which was used only to affirm the infallibility of its visible head; or the suppression of a very active magisterium on the part of Doctors and universities—two facts which were vigorously invoked by the concilarists, at the beginning of the fifteenth century, but in an atmosphere of severance from the papal function and of opposition to it. The victory of the papalists (Turrecremata, Cajetan) over the conciliarists was the triumph of papal authority, without there being any restoration of the true position of Councils, of the college of bishops, of the *Ecclesia* as such, and of "acceptance": values that the Gallicans, on the other hand, were to assert in the name of history.

[23] Cf. St Thomas, *Quodl.* IX, 16; Bonaventure, *De Perfect. evangel.*, q. 2, a. 2 (which does not go beyond "sedes apostolica a solo Deo iudicatur"); cf. S 86–92; M. Schenk, *Die Unfehlbarkeit des Papstes in der Heiligsprechung* (Freiburg [CH], 1965).

IV. From Trent to Vatican II

The Catholic Church had to face up to formidable questioning and attacks: the Protestant Reformation, internal discussions (Gallicanism, Jansenism), revolutions, rationalism and the development of critical scholarship in historical and religious studies. Its principles of identity and faithfulness were those of today: the belief or sense of the Church, tradition, Scripture and hierarchical ministries. The Council of Trent began by reaffirming the Creed of Nicaea-Constantinople as "principium illus, in quo omnes, qui fidem Christi profitentur, necessario conveniunt ac fundamentum firmum et unicum, contra quod portae inferi nunquam praevalebunt" (DSch. 1500; *Concil. Oecumen. Decreta,* Freiburg, 1962, p. 638). Soon afterwards, it formulated its famous decree on the sacred books (the list of the canonical books) and the traditions which were to be accepted, in regard to the Gospel ("tamquam fontem omnis et salutaris veritatis et morum dis-ⁱ ciplinae" (DSch. 1501 ff.). Trent very often appeals to the *"sensus Ecclesiae"*, which it understands in an objective sense: *that which* the Church believes and holds; that which it has always held.[24] There is nothing more traditional.

The Protestant Reformation, however, took the already ancient suit (the anti-ecclesiastical sects, Wycliffe, Huss) favouring Scripture against the excessive weight of ecclesiastical rulings. It tended to locate the principle of unity in Christ alone, in the Word of God, while radically undervaluing the visible mediations and criteria associated with human instances. The invention of printing allowed *Scriptura sola* to be given a concrete effectiveness. The controversy primarily concerned the Rule of Faith. This conditioned the efforts of Catholic apologists and theologians, and helped to orient doctrine in a new direction. The following, sketched in a rather dry form, are the main elements in this story that are relevant to my subject-matter:

(1) The elaboration and systematization of theological criteriology: the *De locis* of Cano appeared in 1562. See A. Lang's

[24] Cf. G, vol. II, pp. 82 and 291; J. Salaverri, *Estud. Eclesiast.,* 1946, pp. 56 ff.; *infra*, n. 27; for the Tridentine teaching concerning tradition, cf. F, vol. I, pp. 207-32. There is no room here to cite the great number of studies published on this subject.

studies. In particular there was to be a focusing on the *positive* qualifications, with such new categories as *sententia probabilis, doctrina tuta, theologice certum, proxima fidei* (!), which were to play a major role in modern mariology, enlivened by the ambition to prepare new dogmatic definitions (cf. Q 24).

(2) The doctrine of apostolicity, which was so important in the second and third centuries (yet so seldom a theme in the Middle Ages), was carefully elaborated with an admittedly non-exclusive though very firm and careful insistence on the apostolicity of the ministry (the "apostolic succession"). The "Roman" mark obtained a kind of "primacy".[25]

(3) The term *dogma* and what it designates came to have a more precise and narrow meaning. It had merely the sense of doctrine, pronouncement, principle, or maxim. It was only in the eighteenth century that it came to be used in its strict modern sense, and in speaking of *such and such* a dogma instead of *dogma* pure and simple, as has been done since then.[26] The notions of *fides* and *haeresis* have undergone a similar process of refinement and restriction of meaning (cf. Q 16 ff.).

The nineteenth century added to the burden of anti-Protestant polemics the emphasis of a "Restoration" atmosphere and of defence against rationalism, secularism, revolutions and subjective thinking. This is expressed in terms of a preoccupation with affirming authority, of magnifying its place and its function, by means of a disregard of individual efforts in thinking, and of the favour extended to a form of neo-Scholasticism as opposed to less strictly rational tendencies (the Roman School, the school-type catechism; and, under Leo XIII, neo-Thomism). In this global context, there are three major facts which deserve notice from our point of view:

(1) The "magisterium" was very actively affirmed. The word in this precise sense comes from the nineteenth century (*Tuas libenter*, 21.12.1863, in regard to the Munich Congress: DSch. 2875 ff.). The unusual activity of the ordinary magisterium of

[25] Cf. G. Thils, *Les Notes de l'Eglise dans l'Apologétique catholique depuis la Réforme* (Gembloux, 1937).

[26] A. Deneffe, "Dogma; Wort und Begriff", *Scholastik* 6 (1931), pp. 381–400; M. Elze, "Der Begriff des Dogmas in der alten Kirche", *Zeitschr. f. Theol. u. Kirche* 61 (1964), pp. 421–38; W. Kasper, *Dogme et Evangile* (Paris, 1967), pp. 28 ff.

the popes (addresses and above all encyclicals) began with Gregory XVI, *Mirari vos*, 15. 8. 1832. There are various degrees of kind and extent of reference of encyclicals: they sometimes offer theology . . . C is a difficult category to define. The Council of 1870 having said nothing precise about the ordinary magisterium of the pope, the faithful (and even some theologians) in fact more or less attributed to it (in the climate of devotion encouraged primarily by the personality of Pius IX) the infallibility which Vatican I had allowed to *ex cathedra* pronouncements. A high point of this exaltation of the ordinary magisterium of the pope was reached under Pius XII and with the encyclical *Humani generis*, 12. 8. 1950 (DSch. 3884–5).

(2) In this issue, there is also some discussion of the dogma of the infallibility of the definitions accorded to the Roman Pontiff and their irrevocable character "ex sese, non ex consensu Ecclesiae". I shall therefore not emphasize here the great theological, ecumenical and historical importance of what was affirmed on 18 July 1870, as the culmination of a "popular" movement and in spite of the opposition of a minority which appealed to history. On the basis of the *infallibility of the Church* (a point that was universally and traditionally accepted), the Council wished to define that the pope is the *subject* or *bearer* of this infallibility in a full sense, being *juridically* independent both of the *ecclesia* and of the rest of the bishops.

(3) In the same year there appeared the *De divina Traditione et Scriptura* of J. B. Franzelin. He accepted, in this vocabulary, the distinction between tradition in the objective sense (the deposit of faith handed down) and tradition in the active sense (the act of transmission).

Franzelin acknowledged the part played by the faithful in the transmission of the deposit of faith, but insisted above all on the main role of the magisterium. At least, that is the point in his teaching that was most developed after him. Scripture and objective or "passive" tradition were made to yield a "distant rule" of faith—the "proximate rule" being the magisterium, very often identified in fact with its Roman instance (on these categories and their arguable content, cf. G, vol. I, pp. 253–4 and 287, n. 84). Hence many theologians operated a kind of reversal of the former position (cf. chapter VI of G, vol. I). This was: the Church (the magisterium) teaches *that which* it believes in order that it may be received. The new position was: that which the Church (the "living magisterium") teaches is a matter of faith, the role of Scripture and tradition being to bear witness to the living magisterium and to justify it. Even a theologian of the value of Scheeben said that to ensure the unity of the Church by means of a recognition of objective truth would be a form of naturalism: the magisterium—and therefore obedience—was necessary. Everything that the ancient Church acknowledged as the absolute truth (and therefore as the infallibility of the belief handed down, received and lived by grace since the apostles) was ascribed to the benefit of the magisterium. The risk was therefore run of attributing to the magisterium an autonomy which it did not possess, and of univocally aligning the *traditio activa* of the deposit of faith with the *traditio activa* of revelation, as made to the apostles (Baumgartner). An analogous process occurred for the idea of *sensus Ecclesiae*: whereas for Trent, it was still the meaning commonly held in the Church, for Vatican I it was the meaning determined by the magisterium as against private judgment.[27] The history of Catholic exegesis, at least up to the encyclical *Divinio afflante* of 30. 9. 1943 (which Pius XII told me, with evident joy, was "liberating"), shows the difficulty of such a programme.

It is not my task here to demonstrate how Vatican II, above all by its dogmatic constitution *Dei Verbum* (far too neglected, unfortunately), re-established a more appropriate equilibrium between revelation and "magisterium", Scripture, tradition, Church and its pastors; still less is it incumbent on me to elucidate the questions raised in the post-conciliar period in regard to the concerns whose history I have traced in such bare outline.

V. Conclusion

The Church has retained and will retain its identity. Its faithfulness transcends the diverse aspects of its history and the way

[27] H. Kümmeringer, "Es ist Sache der Kirche 'iudicare de vero sensu et interpretatione scripturarum sanctarum' "; *Theol. Quartalschr.* 148 (1969), pp. 282-96; cf. also, *ibid.*, pp. 209-34; M. Seckler, "Die Theologie als kirchliche Wissenschaft nach Pius XII. und Paul VI."

in which the very components of this allegiance have been successively or progressively conceived. The role of the theologian, however, is to reflect critically and constructively on these elements, while attempting to realize an ideal of integration. Certain lessons emerge from this history: among them, the following: if the question is to be considered theologically, it is impossible to restrict oneself to *a single* criterion, or to ancient texts without the "living magisterium", or to the living magisterium without the ancient texts, or to authority without the community (cf. Q 37), or to the latter without the former, or to the apostolicity of the ministry without the apostolicity of doctrine, or *vice versa*, or to the Roman Church separated from catholicity, or to the latter detached from the former. . . . All these criteria together should ensure a living faithfulness and identity in the full historicity of our lives and our knowledge. The fullness of the truth is associated with that of the means that God has given us to enable us to live by it; and with the totality of Christian existence.

Translated by John Griffiths

Bibliography

(A) J. A. Möhler, *Die Einheit in der Kirche oder das Prinzip des Katholizismus dargestellt im Geiste der Kirchenväter der drei ersten Jahrhunderte* (1825), Critical ed. by J. R. Geiselmann (Cologne-Olten, 1956).

(B) A. M. Königer, "Prima sedes a nemine judicatur", in *Beiträge z. Geschichte des christlichen Altertums u. der byzantinischen Literatur* (Festgabe A. Ehrhard, Bonn, 1922), pp. 273–300.

(C) D. van den Eynde, *Les Normes de l'Enseignement chrétien dans la littérature patristique des trois premiers siècles* (Gembloux-Paris, 1933).

(D) H. von Campenhausen, *Kirchliches Amt und geistliche Vollmacht in den ersten drei Jahrhunderten* (Tübingen, 1953).

(E) W. Elert, *Abendmahl und Kirchengemeinschaft in der alten Kirche hauptsächlich des Ostens* (Berlin, 1954).

(F) Charles Munier, *Les sources patristiques du Droit de l'Eglise du VIIIe au XIIIe siècle* (Mulhouse, 1957).

(G) Yves Congar, *La Tradition et les traditions* (I. *Essai historique*; II. *Essai théologique*) (Paris, 1960–3).

(H) O. Rousseau, J.-J. von Allmen, B.-D. Dupuy, B. Reynders, P. De Vooght, G. Thils, *et al.*, *L'infaillibilité de L'Eglise* (Cheetogne, 1963).

(I) G. G. Blum, *Tradition und Sukzession. Studien zum Normbegriff des Apostolischen von Paulus bis Irenäus* (Berlin-Hamburg, 1963).

(J) G. Florovsky, "The Authority of the Ancient Councils and the Tradition of the Fathers: An Introduction", in *Glauben, Geist, Geschichte: Festschrift E. Benz* Leiden, 1967), pp. 177–88.

(L) J. Mulders, *Onfeilbaarheid* (Hilversum, 1968).

(M) K. F. Morrison, *Tradition and Authority in the Western Church, 300–1140* (Princeton, 1969).

(N) Yves Congar, *L'Eglise de S. Augustin à l'époque moderne* (*Hist. des Dogmes III/3*) (Paris, 1970).

(O) U. Wickert, *Sacramentum Unitatis: Ein Beitrag zum Verständnis der Kirche bei Cyprian* (Berlin and New York, 1971).

(P) H. J. Sieben, "Zur Entwicklung der Konzilsidee", *Theologie und Philosophie* 45 (1970), pp. 353–89; 46 (1971), pp. 40–70, 364–86.

(Q) P. F. Fransen, "Unity and Confessional Statements: Historical and Theological Inquiry of Roman Catholic Traditional Conceptions", *Bijdragen* 33 (1972), pp. 2–38.

(R) L. Frank, *Der Sinn der Kanonbildung: Eine historisch-theologische Untersuchung der Zeit vom I Clemensbrief bis Irenäus von Lyon* (Freiburg, 1971).

(S) Brian Tierney, *Origins of Papal Infallibility, 1150–1350: A Study on the Concepts of Infallibility, Sovereignty and Tradition in the Middle Ages* (Leiden, 1972).

Truth and Verification at Vatican I

Gustave Thils

I. INFALLIBILITY AND TRUTH

THE sound and fury surrounding the definition of papal infalli-bility in 1870 should not deafen us to the real significance of this event for the everyday life of the Christian. For "infallible" de-finitions, whether by ecumenical councils or popes, are by their very nature infrequent and exceptional, as history, even recent history, clearly shows. The Church, the people of God, believes and goes forward in history under the sign of living and saving truth. As long as nothing arises to disturb the community or to require a solemn definition, there is no reason for the infallible magisterium to be exercised. Infallibility is in the service of the truth, because it is the truth and not fantastic theories (Eph. 4. 14) which is the source of salvation. If the Lord promised his special help in crucial moments, it was to protect the saving truth and not for the glory of a council or a pope. There is a way of speaking about the place of infallible definitions in the Church which obscures their true significance, their significance in the eyes of Christ. *Truth* must remain or be restored in the minds of Catholics to its central position in the economy of salvation.

This inquiry is especially necessary because there are various forces in operation today which make the very idea of infalli-bility hard to accept. The position is even more awkward when this dogma is given a significance far beyond its definition at the Vatican Council. In the sphere of human truth, modesty and moderation require us to admit the relative nature of historical research, the historicity and perfectibility of doctrinal judgments, the dialectical process of the intellectual life, the place of error in scientific research, and so on. This is why the mere mention of infallibility sounds ridiculously pretentious to many contemporary minds. A doctrinal authority which habitually moved in an infallible sphere would be considered, paradoxically, less credible and the magisterium of the Church would lose rather than gain face.

Did the Fathers of Vatican I consider exactly what they were doing? The eschatological dimension as it impinges on daily life was not mentioned by the minority bishops. But they could have recalled that dogma, like Jewish forms of worship (Heb. 8. 5), is only "an image and shadow of heavenly things" and that the "glorious manifestation of our great God and Saviour, Christ Jesus" (Tit. 2. 13) opens for Christian doctrine qualitatively superior insights to what we now perceive. The debates leading up to the Constitution *Dei Filius* did of course mention the Christian mysteries and their understanding. Their conclusion was that the light of revealed truth is analogous with perceptions of the natural order, the connections between them and their relationship with their final object. These analogies, connections and relationships can become clearer, even in the sphere of dogma. The dogmas the Fathers actually had in mind were those concerning the Trinity and christology. "That the understanding of dogma may grow and develop, as history develops, both in the minds of individual Christians and in the Church as a whole..." (*DS* 3020).

They were not referring to the historicity of dogma, in the sense in which the word is used today. They quoted Vincent of Lérins, in particular the well-known passage from his *Commonitorium*, and had in mind merely the possibility of a better understanding of a changeless mystery. They were aware of a sort of historicity of understanding, but did not consider that man himself and the world are an "historical temporal possibility of being".

It is now commonly said that all truth is perfectible; so how is it possible to insist on the definitive and unchangeable nature of dogmatic definitions? I do not wish to discuss here how certain common human assertions are incontestably unchangeable, but would prefer to show how unchangeable dogmatic definitions are at the same time capable of being perfected.

In the first place, no language can escape the common laws of semantics, not even the language of religious thought, however much believers may want to remain true to the sources of their faith. Furthermore, the reality to which dogmatic definitions point is inexhaustible. Cardinal Bea liked to recall that even the encyclical *Humani Generis* declared that revelation contains an inexhaustible treasury of truth, *tot tantosque continet thesauros veritatis ut nunquam reapse exhauriatur* (*AAS*, 42, 1950, 568). As Karl Rahner has said, the terminology of the concise religious formulations intended for the community of believers should express the infinite richness of our faith, but it is too limited to be able to do this.[1]

Dogma is usually concerned with one aspect of this reality, the saving plan of God and its manifestations in history, the cornerstone of which is Jesus Christ. The truth of the Gospel is the truth of a God who gives himself, who can give himself more and more, displaying his power anew in a history punctuated by *kairoi*. Dogma makes explicit the nature of the good news of revelation; it is concerned with *reality*. Of course "if an angel from heaven should preach to you a gospel contrary to that what we preached to you, let him be cursed" (Gal. 1. 8). But this gospel preached by Paul is precisely the gospel of a sovereign Lord who can complete the "new dispensation" that comes to us with Jesus Christ.

We may also add that dogma of course will be perfected when it comes face to face with the full revelation of Jesus Christ. When the epistle to Titus (2. 13) speaks to us of "awaiting our blessed hope, the appearing of the glory of our great God and Saviour Jesus Christ", it opens perspectives for us which will not deny what we already have, but will be qualitatively superior to those offered to us by the Fathers of the early councils in the light they shed on the trinitarian and christological mysteries. We shall only see the total fullness of heavenly glory in the joy of the heavenly Jerusalem: *ad totam aeternae gloriae plenitudinem in coelesti Ierusalem laetus perveniat*. This passage from the Decree on Ecumenism, 3, makes us smile with its

---

[1] K. Rahner, *Qu'est-ce qu'un énoncé dogmatique?* (Ecrits théologiques 7) (Paris, 1967), pp. 230, 234–6.

tota plenitudo, but at least it has the advantage of opening perspectives for us beyond our present understanding.

If we were to ask what conception of the truth governed the decrees of Vatican I we could reply unhesitatingly, an Aristotelian-Platonic one handed down to us by the great medieval scholastics. The identity of being and truth is a fundamental axiom of Platonic philosophy: *verum est id quod est.*[2] The essential position of Aristotelian thought has become well known in the axiom: *veritas est adaequatio rei et intellectus.* And for the medieval theologian, truth is found *proprie et primo* in the divine intelligence, and *improprie et secundario* in us. "Absolute infallibility," declared Mgr Gasser in the name of the deputation on faith, "belongs to God alone, the first and essential truth, who can never in any way deceive us."[3] Should we regret that the notion of truth implied by the Council definitions was not more "modern"? Should it rather have been Kantian, Hegelian or Kierkegaardian? A better knowledge of contemporary philosophy would not have changed the definition of infallibility fundamentally, but it might have been able to forearm the minds of Christians against accepting some of the conciliar preconceptions as absolutes. It might also have helped to stop the development of a theology which misused the doctrines sanctioned by the Council. Finally, it would have helped theologians to approach their material in the different manner appropriate to the different age in which they were living, and that is a necessary part of their task.

II. INFALLIBILITY AND VERIFICATION

What type of verification was adopted by Vatican I? In order to reply to this question, we must distinguish two problems. Firstly, what were the arguments employed by the Council Fathers to justify their "definitive pronouncement" on the infallible magisterium of the Pope? Secondly, what conditions and norms did the Fathers lay down for the exercise of this infallible magisterium to be legitimate and valid? Only the first of these

[2] For what follows see H. Krings, "Verité" in *Encyclopédie de la foi,* IV (Paris, n.d.), pp. 392-5.

[3] See J. D. Mansi, *Sacrorum conciliorum nova et amplissima collectio,* 52, 1214a.

problems concerns us here.[4] The Bishop of Brixen, Mgr Gasser, reviewed the arguments for the last time in his address just before the final vote, saying that revealed truth must be capable of proof by Scripture and tradition and that these proofs had already been carefully considered in the general assemblies. The Fathers' reasoning was, of course, expressed in the dogmatic theology of the time, "Roman", anti-Protestant, out of touch with Orthodox teaching and almost completely disregarding biblical exegesis and history in the modern sense. The Fathers were in fact convinced, although they did not deny the necessity of the arguments, that they, the Council, were sufficient witness and judgment and that the authority of their decisions was guaranteed by the Holy Spirit.

This belief was based on their conviction that they were in continuity with the twelve apostles who received from the Lord, together with their mission to found and rule the Church, the promise of his help till the end of time. "I am with you always, to the close of the age" (Matt. 28. 20). Although they all had the same source, each of the Fathers understood this belief in a different way, varying between those whose enthusiasm suggested the definition of infallibility by acclamation and the stubborn reticence of those who left Rome a few days before the proclamation of the dogma. Of course the Fathers did not wish to canonize the whims of any pope. They laid down conditions necessary to a legitimate definition. They did not reach agreement on the scope of infallible definitions by the Pope, e.g., in theological matters, whether pronouncements by a pope on doctrines "not revealed but closely connected with revelation" could be regarded as infallible.[5] However, they themselves were conditioned by the Counter-Reformation, which stressed the status of the hierarchy and papacy in reaction to Protestant denials; and many of them had been trained in Rome and their theological education was strictly that of the Roman curia.

With regard to verification, the arguments put forward to support the dogmatic definition are urgently in need of revision now. We have already quoted Mgr Gasser as saying that revealed

[4] For the conditions and limitations of the exercise of the pope's infallible magisterium, see G. Thils, *L'infallibilité pontificale. Source, conditions, limits* (Gembloux, 1969), pp. 186–221.

[5] See G. Thils, *op. cit.*, pp. 234–46.

truth must be capable of proof by Scripture and tradition.[6] This "proof" was made on the basis of the exegesis and the history of 1870 or more precisely exegesis and history as summarized in the treatises *De Ecclesia* and *De Romano pontifico* in the parts dealing with papal prerogatives. Even if we accept the conclusions of these manuals today, we cannot say that the quality of nineteenth-century exegesis and history to be found in them is impeccable. We have a fairly extensive and official example of these in Mgr B. d'Avanzo's commentary on Mt. 16. 18, Lk. 22. 32 and Jn. 21. 16–17, in reply to the criticisms of Cardinal Schwarzenburg, Archbishop of Prague.[7] He concluded that the apostles were absolutely and totally dependent on Peter, on the strength of an exegesis which we cannot accept as doing great honour to its authors. What is more, this statement was made in the name of the deputation on faith and was not a merely private view.

More fundamentally, the justification of the Council's definition rests on the Lord's promise. Even if we accept that God will help the Church till the end of time, it is most necessary here to speak with care and moderation or this truth becomes totally unacceptable and the Holy Spirit is compromised by unworthy declarations.

A consideration of the Catholic doctrine of the infallibility of all believers *in credendo* or of the college of bishops *in docendo* will help us understand how necessary it is not to exaggerate the scope of what we are affirming. Post-Tridentine teaching recognizes the infallibility of all believers *in credendo*. Does this mean that they are always right or that a current notion is infallible simply because it is shared by everyone? Of course not. All it means is that a special moment can be known when the whole Christian community confesses its faith unanimously in a doctrine revealed by God. At this moment, we must believe either that Christ's promise is of little value or that the help of the Holy Spirit will at least be manifested in this, namely that an "error" will never be unanimously believed to be "revelation" and that under these conditions everything that is declared to be

[6] J. D. Mansi, *op. cit.*, vol. 52, 1204c.
[7] See J. D. Mansi, *op. cit.*, 52, pp. 713–9. Also G. Thils, *La primauté pontificale. La doctrine de Vatican I. Le voies d'une révision* (Gembloux, 1972), pp. 163–7.

"revealed" and thus "true" is in fact "revealed" and thus of necessity absolutely "true". This is what is *de fide* in the doctrine of the infallibility of the faithful *in credendo*. When the matter concerns truths which are not revealed but are closely connected with revelation, the possibility of infallible judgments is not *de fide* but a theological certainty.

In the same way, believing that the Holy Spirit helps the Pope in the exercise of his supreme magisterium does not mean that in every important act of this magisterium the Holy Spirit will give his full, decisive aid. It would be wrong to imagine that the Saviour's promise of divine help guaranteed every papal declaration. If so, the syllogism would read as follows: The papal magisterium is a divine institution and promised the help of the Holy Spirit. Now the Pope declares such and such. . . . Therefore this truth is guaranteed by God. It is easy to see what is wrong with such an argument. The help of the Spirit is not necessarily always fully effective or guaranteed unconditionally. The light of the Spirit can be dimmed by our darkness, and his power can be thwarted if we resist. In short, the Holy Spirit does not act by magic. Even if we prove his presence, this does not guarantee that he is present in maximum power and light.

Moreover, we should not forget that the help of the Holy Spirit is given for the preservation and faithful transmission of Christian revelation. The further we move from the heart of revelation, the less we can expect the Holy Spirit to guarantee our beliefs. Vatican I excluded the government of the Church from the province of infallibility. In the case of non-revealed truths which are "necessarily connected" and are called the secondary object of infallibility, prudence is strictly required here and it is not *de fide* that the Church or the Pope can make an infallible pronouncement on these matters. Even greater prudence is required in the case of natural law. Is it really possible to rely on the help promised the Church's magisterium to safeguard revelation in order to establish in a precise and technical manner this or that doctrine of property, the rights of the individual or behaviour in married or family life? If we do not observe subtle distinctions, we end by making all kinds of statements absolute, statements which will sooner or later be swept aside or eroded at the expense of faith.

The Constitution *Gaudium et spes* on the Church in the Modern World of Vatican II wisely reminds us that the Church does not always have an immediate answer to every question, and tries to enlist the joint help of the light of revelation and the competence of each individual: *lumen revelationis cum omnium peritia coniugere cupit* (no. 33). When urgent problems are being studied, Vatican II advises us to rely on the "light of the gospel and the human experience of every man" *sub luce Evangelii et humanae experientiae omnium* (no. 46). That is to say that pastors should consider problems in the usual way. The many declarations of *Gaudium et spes* on the legitimate autonomy of society, of the sciences and of human institutions surely mean that we must accept the necessity of a dialogue between the Church and these bodies is a necessity.

In an essay on infallibility ("Réflexions philosophiques sur l'infaillibilité"), M. A. de Waelhens came to this conclusion: "If the idea of infallibility implies a judgment without any risk of error, then the philosopher must reject that idea. But we have shown that truth can be understood on another, higher level. If one accepts the idea of a source of truth, beyond human judgment, the meaning of meaning, and that this original truth is also the source of being, whose nature is to give meaning by understanding being, then one can admit that there is place for human infallibility. I admit I find it difficult to bring these reflections to bear on the immediate subject of this essay. But, although I am no theologian, it is, I think, possible to say that *mutatis mutandis* the light of faith is a gift which opens us to another presence apart from that of the world, and that in this respect it is infallible. But this presence is also an invitation to study and develop theological truth. This theological task does not of course carry the same guarantee. But because it lives in the light of this presence, it can go on without ever losing sight of that presence, which is its measure, but whose measure it can never completely take."[8]

Theologians would benefit by meditating on these reflections.

Translated by Dinah Livingstone

---

[8] E. Castelli, *et al.*, *L'infaillibilité. Son aspect philosophique et théologique* (Paris, 1970), p. 407.

Aspects of the Truth in the New Testament

Jean Giblet

TRUTH is discussed in many different ways in Scripture. How can these texts and the ideas in them help us here, in this number of *Concilium*, in our search for truth and certainty in the Church? Let us begin by examining some important data in the Old Testament and by considering especially the part played by "truth" in the gospel of John and then end with a few suggestions.

I. GREEK IDEAS AND THE HEBREW MIND

It has become customary in recent years to make a systematic distinction between Greek and Hebrew concepts of truth.[1] T. F. Torrance has written that the usual translation of *'emeth* in the Septuagint, *aletheia*, does not mean abstract or metaphysical truth, but truth which is derived from God's faithfulness, the active, effective reality of God in his covenant. God's steadfastness, Torrance points out, is the foundation of all biblical truth.[2] The recent criticisms of linguists like James Barr[3] should make New Testament scholars more cautious in their conclusions. We have only to trace the uses of the word *aletheia* in the Septuagint to see that it is not always used to mean "the reality of God

---

[1] Cf. G. Quell, G. Kittel, R. Bultmann, *Theologisches Wörterbuch zum Neuen Testament*, I, pp. 233, 251; T. Boman, *Das hebräische Deuben im Vergleich mit dem Griechischen* (Göttingen, 1954), pp. 162–4.

[2] T. F. Torrance, "One Aspect of the Biblical Conception of Faith", *Exp. Tim.*, LXVIII (1956–7), p. 114.

[3] J. Barr, *The Semantics of Biblical Language* (Oxford, 1961), pp. 160–205.

in his covenant"! We should be careful not to exaggerate the extent of a particularly rich or characteristic usage of a word. However, it is still true that the two languages express minds which have different ways of thinking about the truth.

Aletheia, Bultmann has suggested, originally referred to a situation or a fact which, in so far as it could be seen or expressed, was fully open to view, to demonstration or explanation and represents the full or real fact.[4] To grasp the truth of a being is to know it as it is, in such a manner that it is fully present to the mind. This definitive and full knowledge is in striking contrast to the fluctuations of opinion (*doxa*). If man is capable of perceiving the truth of things in this way, he is also capable of expressing it, of "speaking the truth". This means that his language is so exact that he can communicate what he has ascertained to be true. This is why the idea of truth is primarily an intellectual category.

We may add that, in certain ancient myths and in Plato, truth exists in a world of eternal ideas which is known by the human mind only as a vague nostalgic memory, so that the quest for truth is the well-born man's reason for living (Gorgias 562d). It requires a rigorous intellectual purification and here below can never attain its final object.[5] Greek thought therefore called *aletheia* the supreme divine and eternal reality. Philosophical investigation is necessary, but truth can also be glimpsed momentarily in ecstasy. In other words full knowledge of the truth is the result of personal mystical experience.[6] This was the ideal followed in certain Greek or Jewish Greek philosophical and religious circles. The early Christians may have been acquainted with them and have tried to define their attitude towards them.

In Hebrew, things are rather different. Etymologically, the word *'emeth,* usually translated, as we have seen, by *aletheia* in the Septuagint means that which is *āmen,* that is to say, firm, solid, sure, a trustworthy foundation. The word is used to de-

---

[4] R. Bultmann, *op. cit.,* p. 239.

[5] M. Detienne, "La notion mythique *d'Alètheia*", *Revue des Etudes Grecques,* LXXIII (1960), pp. 27–35; P. Friedländer, *Platon, Seinswahrheit und Lebenswirklichkeit* (Berlin, 1954), pp. 233 ff.; M. Sauvage, *L'aventure philosophique* (Paris, 1966).

[6] Philo, *De vita Mos.,* II, 128, 271; *Spec. Leg.,* I, 89; *Migr. Abrah.,* I, 76; *Corp. Herm.,* XIII, 6, 9; *Exc. ap. Stob.,* IIa (Scott).

scribe human behaviour and words—a man's word is true if it expresses his thought accurately and a man is true if he keeps his word. The word *'emeth* is often applied to God and refers to his absolute faithfulness to his promises in the covenant: God alone is true in the strongest sense of the word, because he alone truly keeps his word, which he gave in his loving kindness to the children of Israel in the covenant. For his part, man can trust in God, believe in him and express his faith by lasting obedience. To be faithful is to be true, to keep a promise, to keep the covenant. God is absolutely true but man is never absolutely true to the end. We see how truth is connected with trusting faith and justice in Hebrew thought.[7]

God's word can be relied on absolutely. His word is not only a promise or a command, it can also speak his plan, give details of the promise. In Proverbs, God's word is wisdom, what God reveals, the teaching which comes from God to instruct those who believe in him and do his will.[8] In the last resort, truth is also the mystery of God, glimpsed now through grace and revealed on the last day. So knowledge of the truth becomes the object of hope. These usages are particularly characteristic of the later wisdom and apocalyptic writings; they had a profound influence on the Qumran sects.[9] They were also prevalent in the New Testament and especially in Paul[10] and John. I shall concentrate on the latter, because his vision is richer and more complex.

II. The Manifestation of the Truth in John

Everyone agrees on the importance of the idea of truth in the gospel and epistles of John. Many authors, following R. Bultmann and C. H. Dodd, stress the Hellenistic affinities.[11] Others

---

[7] D. Michel, "Amät. Untersuchung über 'Wahrheit' im Hebräischen", *Archiv für Begriffsgeschichte*, 12, 1 (Bonn, 1968), pp. 30–57.

[8] Dan. 10. 21, 11. 2; Wis. 3. 9, 6. 22, Prov. 8. 6.

[9] O. Betz, *Offenbarung und Schriftforschung in der Qumransekte* (Tübingen, 1960), pp. 53–60.

[10] J. Murphy O'Connor, "La 'vérité' chez saint Paul et à Qumran", *Revue Biblique*, LXII (1965), pp. 29–76.

[11] C. H. Dodd, *The Interpretation of the Fourth Gospel* (Cambridge, 1953), pp. 170–8; R. Bultmann, "Untersuchungen zum Johannesevangelium: *Aletheia*", *Zeitschrift für Theologische Wissenschaft*, XXVII

like de la Potterie draw attention to the contacts with Jewish wisdom and apocalyptic writings.[12] In fact, John is full of complications in this respect. He draws on many ideas and unites them by means of the Incarnate Word on which they all converge.

1. In many cases the word truth is associated with speaking or passing on the word: "Now you seek to kill me, a man who has told you the truth which I heard from God" (Jn. 8. 40). The word "truth" like the word "word" is used for the teaching of Jesus as a whole; his teaching passes on the pure and perfect word of God (Jn. 3. 31 f.; 12. 47 f.). Jesus confidently brings the definitive word revealing God's plan to the world and he invites his listeners to believe and obey without doubting. On the other hand, the prince of the world of sin and evil (Jn. 12. 31; 16. 11) is called the inventor of lies. "He was a murderer from the beginning, and has nothing to do with the truth, because there is no truth in him. When he lies, he speaks according to his own nature, for he is a liar and the father of lies" (Jn. 8. 44). This is a dualist idea which recalls the expressions of apocalyptic or Qumran literature, as de la Potterie says. We should note that, to understand truth in the word of Jesus, man must have a certain attitude. Only he who "does the truth" (Jn. 3. 19), "he who is the truth" (Jn. 18. 37) can hear the word of God and believe in it. The assent of faith also requires commitment, obedience which is faithful and lasting (1 Jn. 2. 4 f.; 3. 18 f.). The knowledge of God's truth is a source of freedom because believers become children of God (Jn. 8. 32), and share in God's holiness (Jn. 17. 17 f.). Thus there is a close connection between knowing, doing and being.

2. But Jesus not only passes on what he has heard. He also says what he sees and he manifests the glory of God with whom he is in total communion. Only he can truly see the Father (Jn. 3. 11; 6. 46; 1. 18) and this vision affects his behaviour as man. The

(1928), pp. 113–63; see also A. Wikenhauser, R. Schnackenburg and the slightly different approach of H. Schlier, *Meditationen über den johannischen Begriff der Wahrheit, Festschrift für M. Heidegger* (Pfullingen, 1959), pp. 195–203.

[12] I. de la Potterie, "La verità in San Giovanni", *Atti della XVII Settimana Biblica* (Brescia, 1964), pp. 123–44.

story of the curing of the paralysed man at the pool ends with this word of Jesus: "My Father is working still and I am working" (Jn. 5. 17). Jesus continues, "Truly, truly, I say to you, the Son can do nothing of his own accord, but only what he sees the Father doing; for whatever he does, that the Son does likewise. For the Father loves the Son, and shows him all that he himself is doing (Jn. 5. 19 f.). The works of Jesus are signs manifesting the glory of God to those who have the faith to see (Jn. 2. 11). This is why John lays particular importance on watching and gradually understanding what Jesus' own life and behaviour reveal.[13]

This leads up to the idea that the truth of God is manifest in Jesus Christ. This is how we should understand the central statement of the prologue: "The Word became flesh and dwelt among us, full of grace and truth; we have beheld his glory, glory as of the only Son from the Father. . . . And from his fullness we have all received, grace upon grace" (Jn. 1. 14, 16). It is possible that the oldest part of the prologue was a piece borrowed and expanded by John.[14] The prologue develops some of the above ideas and suggests new aspects. The eternal Son is called the Logos, that is he who in all his being is the perfect expression of the Father (cf. Col. 1. 15; Phil. 2. 6; Heb. 1. 3). By his incarnation he now belongs to this world, he shares our human condition and becomes the full and definitive manifestation of his Father on earth. He who begins to see this manifestation is transformed by it and this perception-participation continually develops (cf. 2 Cor. 3. 17). The formula "grace and truth", well known in Old Testament tradition (Ex. 34. 6), is connected here with the theme of the glory of God. "Grace and truth" is given the wider meaning of manifestation of God himself who graciously transforms those who are ready to receive him. This is what brings the new world to replace the Mosaic era. The law was given by Moses, grace and truth come through Jesus Christ. No one has ever seen God. His only Son who abides in the bosom of the Father has declared him (Jn. 1. 17–18).

[13] Cf. H. Wenz, "Sehen und Glauben bei Johannes", *Theologische Zeitschrift*, 17 (1961), pp. 17–25; C. Traets, *Voir Jésus et le Père en lui selon l'Evangile de S. Jean* (Rome, 1967).
[14] Cf. R. Schnackenburg, "Logos-Hymnus und johanneischer Prolog", *Biblische Zeitschrift*, I (1957), pp. 69–109.

This is how John 14. 6 ff. should, in my opinion, be read:
"I am the way, and the truth, and the life; no one comes to the
Father, but by me. If you had known me, you would have known
my Father also; henceforth you know him and you have seen
him. . . . He who has seen me has seen the Father; how can you
say 'Show us the Father'? Do you not believe that I am in the
Father and the Father in me?" (Jn. 14. 6–7, 9–10). Because, as
the Son, Jesus is the one who comes from the Father and returns
to him, he is also the one who in all his human behaviour shows
the Father. Jesus is the truth not only by the words he speaks,
but also by his history, of which the disciples are witnesses; thus
faith is knowledge and vision, never complete, of the Father in
him.

3. So the truth of God is revealed through the humanity of
Jesus Christ and it is most clearly revealed in the Easter events
(cf. Jn. 12. 23 ff.; 13. 31–2; 17. 1 ff.). Everyone is confronted
directly or indirectly with these events. But for John, seeing requires penetration, the ability to read progressively the meaning
of certain signs and this is the work of the Holy Spirit, himself
the result of Easter (Jn. 7. 37–9; 16. 5). The texts about the Spirit
of truth or the Paraclete in the great discourses (which John puts
in the middle of the Easter events) are particularly important
here. We can only remind ourselves of the principal passages.[15]
"When the Counsellor comes, whom I shall send to you from
the Father, even the Spirit of truth who proceeds from the
Father, he will bear witness to me; and you also are witnesses
because you have been with me from the beginning" (Jn. 15.
26–7). Thus the Paraclete is the disciples' sure support, because
he proceeds from the truth and can lead them to the knowledge
of the truth. This truth is in Jesus, his life, work and word. The
mission of the Spirit is to lead the disciples to a gradual understanding of the truth manifest in Jesus. They will discover the
full meaning of what they have heard and seen. "The Counsellor,
the Holy Spirit whom the Father will send in my name, he will

[15] Bibliography to article "Pneuma", *Theologisches Wörterbuch zum
Neuen Testament*, pp. 330 ff.; O. Betz, *Der Paraklet* (Arbeiten zur
Geschichte des Spätjudentums und Urchristentums, 2) (Leiden and
Cologne, 1963); G. Johnston, *The Spirit-Paraclete in the Gospel of John*
(Cambridge, 1970).

teach you all things, and bring to your remembrance all that I have said to you" (Jn. 14. 26). "I have yet many things to say to you, but you cannot bear them now. When the Spirit of truth comes, he will guide you into all the truth; for he will not speak on his own authority, but whatever he hears he will speak, and he will declare to you the things that are to come. He will glorify me, for he will take what is mine and declare it to you" (Jn. 16. 12–14). Thus the work of the Spirit of truth is to lead to the discovery of Christ. He will show the true meaning of the life and words of Jesus. All revelation is in him and the Spirit is to lead the disciples to understand Christ who is the key to the saving plan of God.

4. He is not talking of disciples merely, but means apostles, those who were with him from the beginning (Jn. 15. 27; cf. Acts 1. 21) and so become his witnesses. These apostles have just received their commission (Jn. 15. 14–16; 17. 17–21; 20. 21 ff.). By their witness which will echo the witness of the Spirit, they will create the place where the truth will be accessible to believers (Jn. 12. 21). Of course the gift of the Spirit is not for the apostles alone, but as they shared the earthly life of Jesus, the Spirit works in them in a special way, so that they may bear witness which can be trusted by future believers. The whole schema is very complicated. The gradual discovery of the truth is the work of the Spirit, but this discovery is made through the witness of the apostles as received and understood by the Church.

Some of these testimonies, and in particular that of the beloved disciple, will be written down. The Church which receives them is capable of recognizing their truth (Jn. 19. 35; 21. 24). These written testimonies do not exhaust the understanding of the fullness of revelation in Jesus, but they fix for ever the essential structure. To understand is to belong to the apostolic tradition guarded and lived by the Church.[16] The *proagon* (2 Jn. 9) "he who goes ahead and pretends to be in advance of the apostolic tradition does not abide in the doctrine of Christ and does not have God" (2 Jn. 9). In fact, as F. Mussner notes, he has his own previous

---

[16] We could have developed here the meaning of truth as "sound doctrine" and the "paratheke" in the pastoral epistles. Cf. J. Roloff, *Apostolat-Verkündigung-Kirche* (Gütersloh, 1965), pp. 244–9; A. T. Hanson, *Studies in the pastoral epistles* (London, 1968), pp. 5–20.

understanding and preconception of Christ but he holds that the "hermeneutical circle" of the apostolic tradition is also a vicious circle. In his exegesis he makes use of other traditions, philosophical or mythical traditions, for example. His Christ is thus a completely new figure, essentially different from tradition and even contrary to it. This is just what John never does. He has his "prejudice" which colours his interpretation of Christ from the christological tradition preceding the Church.[17] There is no true understanding except in continuity with the apostolic tradition and the Spirit of truth is the principal and final norm for this understanding from the beginning to the last day. These considerations are the necessary introduction to the question of formulas of faith, which the Church of course needs, but which must never be regarded as norms expressing once and for all the definitive truth of revelation. There is no end to the discovery of God in Jesus Christ.

Translated by Dinah Livingstone

[17] F. Mussner, *The Historical Jesus in the Gospel of John* (Freiburg/London, 1967) (*Die johanneische Sehweise*, Freiburg im Br., 1965).

The Person and Office of Peter in the New Testament

Josef Blank

I INTEND in this essay to try to broaden discussion of the "Petrine office" by the addition of certain new exegetical and hermeneutical considerations, in the hope that these may perhaps be useful in opening up positions that are still very rigid. I should like to refer readers to R. Pesch's article, "The Position and Significance of Peter in the Church of the New Testament"[1] and to the sources

[1] *Concilium* (April 1971), pp. 21–35 (American Edn., vol. 64).

cited there. I am largely in agreement with him, and especially with the following statement: "The discussion concerning the position and significance of Peter in the New Testament, which in general has concentrated on Matthew 16. 17–19, must be freed from the all too narrow restrictions which have hitherto been imposed on it as a result of treating it merely as a question of the Petrine office and succession."[2] I too consider this to be the central problem. But how is it to be dealt with?

I. HERMENEUTICAL CONSIDERATIONS

1. The examination of office in the Church leads almost at once to a series of difficulties. The New Testament provides us with a highly complicated structure, consisting of a plurality of offices, unsystematic, incomplete and still very fragmentary. But the most likely picture is still of an historical structure. This emerges fairly clearly from the Pauline and the Lucan traditions, but less so from the Matthaean and Johannine traditions. It is also true of the Petrine tradition, despite our faulty knowledge of the person of Peter.[3] The Pauline sources (Gal., 1 Cor.) are the most informative. It is true that Peter is often referred to in the four gospels as "spokesman" of the apostles or shown with James and John as the chosen witness on special occasions. But these instances do not tell us a great deal about him personally, because they are very largely concerned with Peter as a "type" and not with the historical Peter.

It is even more important to keep this in mind when we read Luke's Acts of the Apostles, for the speeches by Peter recorded there are really to be seen as Luke's own creation.[4] They are no more valuable as sources of a "Petrine theology" than the two pseudonymous letters of Peter.[5] We know absolutely nothing

[2] *Op. cit.*, p. 32.
[3] See Pesch, *op. cit.*, pp. 25 ff., the section entitled "Specific Historical Questions".
[4] M. Dibelius, *Die Reden der Apostelgeschichte und die antike Geschichtsschreibung, Aufsätze zur Apostelgeschichte* (Göttingen, 4th edn., 1961), pp. 120–62; U. Wilckens, *Die Missionsreden der Apostelgeschichte* (Neukirchen, 2nd edn., 1963).
[5] O. Cullmann, on the other hand, believes that the basic elements of a Petrine theology can be found. He sees it in "universalism" and in a christology based on the suffering servant of Yahweh, especially as it

about the theology advocated by the historical Peter, though it cannot have been very different from the Judaeo-Christian theologies of the early Christian communities.

The increasingly frequent references in the New Testament to Peter as a "type" or "symbol" merits special attention. If the Petrine office receives any mention at all in the New Testament, then it is surely in this problematical area. In this case our question should be formulated thus: How did the "historical" Peter come to be a Petrine "type"? What does this "type" represent? What is the special symbolic value of the person of Peter?

2. We may therefore assume that it was less the historical Peter, and much more the symbolical or even the "mythical" Peter, who made history. I am here using the word "mythical", not as it is used in the history of religion, but in its sociological and historical sense. Great historical developments like those emanating from Peter are simply not possible without the creation of myths, types and symbols.

It is true, of course, that a core of historical truth always underlies such symbols. The symbols, however, soon acquire a much greater power of attraction than the historical facts. In the case of Peter, we are all the more justified in considering his symbolic significance, since the name Kephas or "Rock", which was given to the fisherman Simon from Bethsaida either by Jesus himself, as I am inclined to believe, or by the primitive community, as others believe,[6] is in any case a symbolic name that points to a symbolic function.

Anticipating questions about this explanation, I would point to the fact that symbols invariably contain a variety of possible meanings and interpretations. A symbol is diminished if one single interpretation is held to be the only possible one. Similarly, an exclusively juridical approach often lacks the imaginative content and fullness of meaning of a symbol.

In the New Testament, then, Peter came to have both positive and negative characteristics. On the one hand, he was the apostle

---

appears in 1 Pet. Cf. *Petrus, Jünger-Apostel-Märtyrer* (Stuttgart, 2nd edn., 1960), pp. 72-7; and the same author's *Die Christologie des Neuen Testaments* (Tübingen, 1957), p. 74.

[6] E.g., R. Pesch, *op. cit.*, pp. 26-7. "Symbolic name" is more suitable than "honorific name".

who confessed the Messiah (Mark 8. 27–30), to whom, according to Matthew 16. 17–19, Luke 22. 31 f. and John 21. 15–17, great things were promised and to whom, according to 1 Cor. 15. 5, the risen Lord first appeared. He also led the early Church after Easter and courageously preached Christ to the world outside. But on the other hand he was also the disciple whom Jesus castigated as "Satan" (Mark 8. 31–33), who was described in the allegorical story of the sinking ship as a doubter and waverer, a man of little faith (Matthew 14. 28–31), who denied Jesus (Mark 14. 29–31; 53–54; 66–72) and who was corrected by Paul at Antioch (Gal. 2. 11–16). It is curious that this combination of positive and negative characteristics is found wherever the Petrine tradition occurs in the New Testament. This might point to a "core of historical truth". Ancient tradition is completely free of a one-sided glorification of Peter. Unfortunately the positive side of Petrine symbolism was often given a one-sided emphasis later, whereas its negative side was played down or silently ignored.

3. We must now consider the emergence of "office" in the Church. No doubt because of the expectation of an immediate *parousia*, the early Church never thought of forming a structure, consisting of many offices of the type that would be required by a more long-term institution. The familiar view that Jesus' sole intention had been to found a Church and to furnish it as completely as possible with all the necessary powers and offices belongs to the realm of dogmatic thought. Historically, it can no longer be justified. That is to say, the problems of "succession" of office-holders, whether of the "Apostles", the "Twelve" or even "Peter", simply did not exist in the early Church. Where these problems appear, as in the pastoral letters, or in an early form in Luke's Acts (Acts 20: Paul's farewell speech in Miletus), they come at a relatively late stage, towards the end of the first century.

What we now have to consider, however, are the requirements of a far longer period. And we must deal with the problems involved in an entirely new, independent and previously unforeseen way. To do so we have to turn to the existing community tradition handed down by Paul and especially by Jesus. But now we can see that this tradition is far less concerned with "office" and "succession" and far more with the protection and safe-guarding of its own continuity. The "succession" problem only appeared when the early Church realized the necessity of preserving and defending this tradition against misinterpretation.

Closely linked to the concept of tradition is that of succession as a way of rationalizing and legitimizing, for post-apostolic generations, their relationship to the early Church. It is no accident that the second and third centuries A.D. were the period in which the "forms" of the early Catholic and universal Church were established, especially the monarchical and episcopal forms, and the first attempts made to secure for Rome the role of leadership.[7] But these developments were far less dogmatic and far more pragmatic than the subsequent theology of Irenaeus and Eusebius.

At this point we must turn to the findings of C. Andresen in his recent book on the ancient Christian churches.[8] Andresen lays special stress, and rightly, on the importance of taking into account the sociological, political and cultural factors that played a part in the evolution of office in the Church.[9] If we ignore these sociological and cultural questions, we shall not have a proper historical understanding of the Church and this will in turn affect our dogmatic and our biblical understanding of the problem.

If we go back in history to the New Testament, then we must have the courage to see the historical gaps and to recognize historical changes. On the other hand, Christian exegesis can make meaningful statements, even in a framework divorced from its sources, about its understanding of office and about the form

[7] Cf. G. Bardy, *La Théologie de l'Eglise de saint Irénée au concile du Nicée* (Paris, 1947); Mirbt-Aland, *Quellen zur Geschichte des Papsttums und des römischen Katholizismus* I (Tübingen, 6th edn., 1967).

[8] C. Andresen, *Die Kirchen der alten Christenheit* (Stuttgart, 1971).

[9] See Andresen, *op. cit.*, p. 10. "What we think of as the 'type' of the Church only developed in the dialectical relationship between the Church's own self-awareness and the sociological, political and cultural factors of the history of those times." With regard to the first letter of Clement, Andresen is of the opinion that "the hierarchy of elders, despite its transformation in East and West, was the characteristic structure of office in the early Church. This also raises the question of the factors that determined the quality of Christian communities in the early Church. If we do not consider the sociological factors, we shall not do justice to the data in the second century" (p. 56).

and unique function of the early Christian diaconate, that is to say, the special theological, christological, ecclesiological and moral aspects of "office". It will then be seen that, if there is any predominant and universal principle, it is first and foremost that of the unconditional headship of Christ in the whole of the Church's life and work, the lordship of the *Kyrios* and the continuing and all-embracing authority of Jesus.[10]

I have thought it worth while to deal with these points at some length because problems of this nature form part of the current argument, and have to be brought to the surface. R. Pesch has himself already drawn attention to the fact that we can make no progress with a straightforwardly biblical argument of the "pro" and "contra" sort.[11]

II. NEW TESTAMENT MODELS FOR THE FIGURE OF PETER

We must try, in this section, to discover certain basic characteristics of the figure of Peter in the New Testament, characteristics that might be theologically relevant to our problem.

1. *Paul: the Authority of Peter and the Absolute Pre-eminence of the Gospel*[12]

We shall begin with Paul because he belonged to the first generation of witnesses who had direct knowledge of the reported facts. Paul provides us with the most important evidence of the Aramaic use of the symbolic name Kephas or "Rock" (1 Cor. 1. 12; 3. 22; 9. 5; 15. 5; Gal. 1. 18; 2. 9, 11, 14. He uses the word *Petros* only twice, in Gal. 2. 7 and 8, probably quoting from the Greek version of the Jerusalem decree on unity).

After Easter, and this is Paul's own period, Simon Peter became the authoritative leader of the primitive community at Jerusalem, most probably because of the Lord's appearance to him at Easter. This authoritative position was completely ac-

---

[10] For the normative authority of Jesus, see K. H. Ohlig, *Woher nimmt die Bibel ihre Authorität?* (Düsseldorf, 1970), pp. 98 f.

[11] R. Pesch, *op. cit.*, p. 32.

[12] The term "gospel" was even in the earliest times used as a technical abbreviation and this is how I use it here; see the fundamental work of P. Stuhlmacher, *Das paulinische Evangelium I, Vorgeschichte* (Göttingen, 1968), pp. 286 ff.

cepted by Paul. Kephas was the leading apostle. Apart from 1 Cor. 15. 5, Paul makes no mention of the "Twelve". Even though his purpose in Gal. 1 and 2 is an apologetic one, the justification of his gospel of "deliverance from the law", and is closely linked to his mission to the Gentiles (cf. Gal. 1. 1 ff.), which was independent of Jerusalem and relied on no human source, he intends in no sense to disparage the first apostle, but to show that his own gospel was recognized by Peter.

Three years after his conversion or vocation, he journeyed to Jerusalem in order to make personal contact with Peter. He stayed fourteen days with him on that occasion (Gal. 1. 18 f.), and one imagines that even on this first visit Paul was concerned with the gospel and anxious to reach agreement with Kephas, which certainly included awareness of Peter's authority. But we must understand the concept of authority in a very loose sense here.

The second visit to Jerusalem took place fourteen years later (Gal. 2. 1–10: Acts 15) on the occasion of the Apostolic Council. The scriptural passage reads as follows: "I went up by revelation; and I laid before them the gospel which I preach among the Gentiles; but privately before those who were of repute, lest somehow I should be running or had run in vain" (Gal. 2. 2). What Paul was striving for at the time was a consensus of opinion between himself and the original Twelve on the subject of the gospel. And in this he was successful (Gal. 2. 6–10). His mission to the Gentiles was accepted. On the other hand, Peter is seen to be the man chiefly responsible for the Jews (Gal. 2. 7 f.). We cannot agree that, after his departure from Jerusalem, Peter submitted to James's jurisdiction.[13] The followers of Jesus, mentioned in Gal. 2. 12, were surely more conservative than the man they claimed to follow.

Paul's acceptance of Peter was not unqualified, however, as is shown by the episode at Antioch (Gal. 2. 11–14; 15–20). This episode was brought about by Peter's unfortunate behaviour, and nearly led to a break between Jewish and Gentile Christians, a division, as Schlier has said, at the Lord's table.[14] Paul's sharp reaction serves only to underline Peter's authority; it would be an incomprehensible reaction on the part of a less influential mem-

[13] I do not agree here with Cullmann, *Petrus, op. cit.*, pp. 46 ff.
[14] Schlier, *Der Brief an die Galater* (Göttingen, 4th edn., 1965), pp. 83 ff.

ber of the community. Paul's accusation of Peter and the Jewish Christians with him was that they "were not straightforward about the truth of the gospel" (Gal. 2. 14). This was their "dissimulation". It is clear that, for Paul, the gospel was of incomparable greatness, and against it could be measured the behaviour of Peter.

Peter had thus offended against the gospel and the spirit of the Jerusalem decree, and this was what Paul accused him of. The attempts both of the Church Fathers and of modern thinkers such as J. Daniélou[15] to justify Peter's behaviour by talk of "economy" or "pastoral reasons" simply does not correspond with the facts. What kind of pastoral care would risk the unity of the community by sacrificing the gospel for the sake of one particular group?

The scanty references to Peter in 1 Cor. are very similar. In Corinth, too, there was a "Petrine" party (1 Cor. 1. 12). Since Peter was probably never in Corinth, this group must have consisted of Jewish Christians, who claimed Peter as the founder of their community. This does not mean, however, that they were unable to claim a higher authority for themselves. For these people, too, Christ was the sole authority. "Is Christ divided?" asks Paul (1 Cor. 1. 13). In 1 Cor. 3. 21 ff. we read: "So let no one boast of men. For all things are yours, whether Paul or Apollo or Cephas or the world or life or death or the present or the future, all are yours; and you are Christ's; and Christ is God's."

It is clear, then, that Paul recognized Peter's authority, though in the sense of *auctoritas* and not as *potestas*. Peter's authority was not exclusive, however, for he shared it with the other "pillars" as *primus inter pares*.

It seems, then, that Peter had very little influence in Paul's missionary field. His influence, according to historical tradition, was far greater in the Jewish Christian sphere. Paul sought agreement with Peter and the first apostles for the sake of the gospel. The gospel or, more concretely, Jesus as *Kyrios* was the absolute

[15] F. Overbeck, *Über die Auffassung des Streits des Paulus mit Petrus in Antiochen (Gal. 2. 11 ff.) bei den Kirchenvätern*, originally published in 1877 (new edition Darmstadt, 1968); J. Daniélou, "Von den Anfängen bis zum Konzil von Nicäa", in Rogier, Aubert and Knowles, eds., *Geschichte der Kirche* I (Einsiedeln, 1963), pp. 60 ff.

authority which could be summoned in extreme cases of dispute even against Peter himself.

2. *Matthew: Peter as Rock of the Church*

We can omit, for the purpose of our argument, the tradition of Mark, because it is not as informative about Peter as it would probably have been had Mark been the pupil and interpreter of Peter. In Mark's account, Peter's confession is so closely linked with the sharp rebuke directed at him by Jesus (Mark 8. 27–33) that we cannot regard this text as an instance of the glorification of Peter. But on the matter of Mt. 16. 13–20, we may assume, since Vögtle's trail-blazing treatment,[16] that Matthew's version was dependent on Mark's, that Matthew 16. 17–19 is a subsequent insertion, and that the text does not refer to the *giving* of a name, but to the *interpretation* of a name.

We must therefore regard Matthew's text as an edited version of Mark's. Matthew has altered Mark's version of the solemn confession of Christ. The formula "Thou art Christ, the Son of the Living God" was intended by Matthew to be a complete statement of who Jesus was (cf. also Matthew 26. 63 and Mark 14. 61). Jesus' answer (verses 17–19) thus corresponds exactly to Peter's confession. It consists of three parts: (a) a blessing; and (b) a twofold promise—(1) the rock on which the Church is to be built (verse 18); and (2) the power of the keys and the power to "bind" and "loose" (verse 19).

When we come to analyse this text, we must be aware not only of Matthew's editorship but of the entire gospel of Matthew as context. Then we shall see certain important parallels. The blessing can be compared with the prophetic words in Matthew 11. 25–27; the word "rock" with the parable of the right way to build a house (Matthew 7. 24–27) at the end of the Sermon on the Mount; the "power of the keys" with the misuse of the keys by the scribes and pharisees (Matthew 23. 13); and finally the power of binding and loosening, with Matthew 18. 18, where this power is given to the whole community.

Seen against the background of these Matthaean parallels, the text in Matthew 16. 17–19 is far from standing alone, as it might

[16] A. Vögtle, "Messiasbekenntnis und Petrusverheissung", *Biblische Zeitschrift*, New Series 1 (1957), pp. 252–72; 2 (1958), pp. 83–103.

at first seem. The blessing in verse 17 points to Peter, in the light
of his confession of Christ, as receiver of the divine revelation,
and as witness to this revelation. To the evangelist, Peter's function was clearly important. As a witness to right faith in Jesus
the Messiah, he is made the foundation rock of the Church of
Jesus. It is a matter, as we have already noted, of the interpretation of a name. What is described is Peter's function in the
Church, as seen by Matthew and his community—the function
of being the foundation. But this function can hardly be thought
of as something to be handed down. For a foundation is only
laid once and on it one continues to build. There is no mention
of a "successor". And the logic of the symbolism allows of no
extension of this particular function.[17]

To infer from this passage that Peter had a "successor" would
be to stretch the interpretation beyond the literal sense of the
symbolism. It is different with the power of the keys and the
power of binding and loosening. If the power of the keys is
regarded as a symbol of the human householder seen in the
light of the Kingdom of God, then the terms "binding" and
"loosening" clearly derive from the rabbinical tradition, where
they refer both to teaching and to communal discipline. We have
to think of both.[18]

It is clear that the Matthaean community used certain elements
of Jewish rabbinical practice and terminology to define its own
powers of teaching and discipline, but that these were made to
conform to Jesus' teaching.[19] If we are right in thinking that
Matthew 18. 18 has to be understood in the light of Matthew

[17] Cf. R. Pesch, op. cit., p. 31.
[18] H. von Campenhausen, Kirchliches Amt und geistliche Vollmacht in
den ersten drei Jahrhunderten (Tübingen, 1953), pp. 135 ff., especially
p. 138. In his view "the two meanings are closely connected. The 'teaching'
of the Church is not a one-sided dogmatic concept—it also includes moral
teaching." R. Hummel, in Die Auseinandersetzung zwischen Kirche und
Judentum im Matthäusevangelium (Munich, 1963), pp. 62 ff., thinks dif-
ferently. He sees Matthew 18. 18 as more concerned with discipline,
Matthew 16. 19 more with teaching: "As possessor of the power to teach,
he was the rock on which the Church of Christ was built", p. 63. See
also G. Bornkamm, "Die Binde- und Lösegewalt in der Kirche des
Matthäus", in Geschichte und Glaube, II (Munich, 1971), pp. 37–50 and
46 ff. and R. Pesch, op. cit., pp. 28 ff.
[19] Cf. R. Hummel, op. cit., pp. 59 ff.

16. 19,[20] then we must conclude that whereas the function of foundation cannot be handed down, the power to bind and loose is seen in Matthew to be transferable to the *entire community*. Thus Peter is seen, both as the one and only foundation of the Church and as a type of the Church and the power given to the Church from Jesus. Peter is therefore the guarantor of right teaching in view of his "confession" and of right practice.[21]

It therefore becomes clear that Matthew 16. 17–19 does not refer to a saying of the earthly Jesus. Even the description "word of the Risen Lord" lacks fullness of meaning. What we have here is a relatively late formation that received its final approval in the Gospel of Matthew. This shows that there already existed a clearly formulated Petrine typology. According to this Judaeo-Christian view, Peter was the foundation of the Church of Jesus, that is to say, the one who received, witnessed to, and guaranteed the original tradition of Jesus. He was also the symbol and type *par excellence* of "apostolic" power in the Church.

In Matthew, then, the Church's power can all be seen as belonging to the "Petrine office", and its subsequent development as simply an unfolding of this power. I believe this to be a possible interpretation. But, according to Matthew, the Church's power is a limited one. It is totally at the service of the teaching handed down by Jesus. It is only a means, not an end in itself. Its purpose is the continuing return to the one Lord and teacher, Jesus Christ, by comparison with whom all others are "pupils" and "brothers" (Matthew 23. 8–10).

The passage in John's final chapter (21. 15–17), which also deals with the handing on of power in the form of pastoral office,

[20] R. Pesch, *op. cit.*, pp. 28 ff., with reference to W. Trilling. I am doubtful whether Matthew 18. 18 can be seen simply as a "later tradition". That Matthew 18. 18 is later editorially is undisputed. I believe that in Matt. 16. 19, what is justified through Peter is a later tradition in the sense of an already existing community practice and, in Matt. 18. 18, this community practice is then justified in the light of the previous justification.

[21] Hummel, Bornkamm and R. Pesch—see note 18—all overlook or underestimate the significance attached in the Matthaean context to Peter's confession of Christ. In verse 17 ἀπεκὰ λυψεν underlines Peter's function as the receiver of revelation in the sense of Matthew 11. 27 and as the witness of revelation. Matthew traces Peter's teaching back to "revelation" just as the rabbis referred the Torah back to the commandments given in Sinai.

has also to be seen in the light of a Petrine typology. In the figure of Peter, the function of "office" is made visible, as the "feeding of the sheep of Jesus" by his shepherd. The explicit reference to the sheep of *Jesus* does away with any claim to lordship in this service (cf. also 1 Peter 5. 2).

Luke 22. 31 f. also fits easily into the same framework, the emphasis being on the strengthening of faith. It presents us with an interpretation—Luke's own—of the rock symbolism. It points to the unfailing, rock-like faith of Peter, but makes clear that Peter owes the firmness of his faith not to his own strength but, in typically Lucan language, to the prayer of Jesus.

But this can hardly have taken place *before* Easter. Peter's speeches in Acts show clearly how, in the concrete, Luke thought of Peter strengthening his brethren, and they aptly illustrate the comparison to "fishers of men" (Luke 5. 1–11).

3. The First and Second Letters of Peter as early Evidence of a Petrine Tradition in Rome[22]

The first letter of Peter is, as we know, based on Pauline tradition. This is especially clear in 1 Peter 2. 13–17, where the author advocates an attitude to the Roman governor which so closely resembles Romans 13. 1–7 that it can almost be taken as a commentary on it. We also find, however, certain original theological ideas. Exhortations to baptism are linked with teaching about suffering closely dependent on a christology of the servant of God,[23] and therefore most probably influenced by Judaeo-Christian tradition and with a series of sayings in which one can recognize the beginnings of early Christian apologetics. What is more, certain formulations about the public behaviour of Christians acquire greater depth if we compare them with the well-known letter of Pliny to Trajan.[24]

[22] R. Knopf, *Die Briefe Petri und Judä* (Göttingen, 1917); H. Windisch and H. Preisker, *Die katholischen Briefe* (*Handbuch zum Neuen Testament 15*) (Tübingen, 3rd edn., 1951); W. G. Kümmel, *Einleitung in das Neue Testament* (Heidelberg, 1963), pp. 303-10, 313-17; Andresen, *Die Kirchen der alten Christenheit, op. cit.*, pp. 58 ff.

[23] Cullmann showed a correct appreciation of this in his *Christologie, op. cit.*, pp. 73 ff.

[24] C. Plini Caecili Secundi, *Epistularum Libri Decem*, ed. Mynors (Oxford, 1963), X, 96, pp. 338 ff.

Is it pure chance that these writings were addressed to small communities in Asia Minor, among them groups in Pontus and Bithynia, where the younger Pliny was Roman governor from 110 B.C. onwards? Where did these writings come from? The code word "Babylon" in the salutation at the end (1 Peter 5. 13) is usually thought to refer to Rome.[25] The persecution situation referred to is surely not Nero's but a later persecution, perhaps Domitian's (A.D. 90–95). It might, however, have been a local persecution.[26]

The reference to Peter as the pseudonymous author could similarly point to Rome, like the christology based on the suffering servant, to which there is an interesting parallel in the first letter of Clement (1 Clement 16). The words "I exhort the elders among you, as a fellow elder" (1 Peter 5. 1) assume that an office of elders or presbyters existed in Rome at the end of the first century. Looked at in this way the first letter of Peter could therefore be early evidence of a Petrine tradition in Rome, and in some people's view bears a close relationship to the first letter of Clement.

I myself also consider the second letter of Peter, which E. Käsemann in his treatise *Eine Apologie der urchristlichen Eschatologie* describes as the "most dubious of the canonical writings", to be part of the Roman Petrine tradition.[27] The issues examined by Käsemann are not the relevant ones here. Moreover, the letter shows clear traces of belonging to the canon. The synoptic tradition and the letters of Paul are both known to the author who makes reference to them (2 Peter 1. 16–19; cf. Matthew 17. 1–9; 3. 14–17). The warning against private interpretation of Scripture (2 Peter 1. 20 f.) is an early indication of a "teaching office" and of the authoritative interpretation of Scripture and the exhortation against Pauline understanding (2 Peter 3. 14–17) could be directed against Marcion, or in general against all false teachers or gnostics.

[25] Cf. also Rev. 14. 8; 16. 19; 17. 5; 18. 2 ff.; and Kümmel, *Einleitung, op. cit.*, p. 309.
[26] For this question see J. Moreau, *Die Christenverfolgung im römischen Reich* (Berlin, 1961), pp. 26 ff.
[27] E. Käsemann, *Exegetische Versuche und Besinnungen* I (Göttingen, 1960), pp. 135–57.

All this brings us well into the middle of the second century, the problems of which period are fully discussed in 2 Peter almost up to the time of the Muratorian Canon. All the facts point clearly to Rome. If we are right in these hypotheses, then we must conclude that Rome, under the symbol of Peter, quickly became the focal point for early Catholic developments.

III. Conclusion

Do we find evidence of a Petrine office in the New Testament? The answer is both yes and no. It is "no" if we search the New Testament for the establishment of the primacy of Rome—this was due to various cultural and historical developments which could not have been foreseen in the early days of the Church. But the answer is also "yes" in the much wider sense of the symbolic point of departure perhaps of ecclesiastical office as a whole, for the purpose of witnessing to the authentic tradition of Jesus, safeguarding it and making continuous renewal in teaching and practice possible. Seen in this way, Peter can perhaps be understood as the "type" of the unity of the Church. But over and above this, he remains the "rock", witnessing to the unique origin of the Church in Jesus Christ.

Translated by Erika Young

II. Interdisciplinary Considerations

Certainty, Truth and the Church's Teaching Office

Iring Fetscher

IN THIS article I shall attempt to throw some light on the meaning of the Catholic concept of infallibility from the vantage point of the relationship between certainty and truth as outlined by Hegel in his *Phenomenology of the Mind*.[1]

I. THE DIALECTICS OF "LORDSHIP AND BONDAGE"

Certainty is the intellectual state of an individual who is completely confident about some matter, knowledge or duty. In his *Phenomenology* Hegel stresses the totally "inward" character of certainty—the way in which a person is certain, for example, of his own "humanity" in the sense of his "superiority over nature" or "intelligence". But this certainty is not an objectively verifiable truth. However great his certainty, a man can only attain to the truth by way of other men—or at least one other man. For Hegel, man's certainty of his own humanity can only be objectively verified through recognition by other human beings. For the acceptance of truth in its existential sense, Hegel requires the presence both of inner certainty and outward recognition of the

---

[1] G. W. F. Hegel, *The Phenomenology of the Mind*, translated by J. B. Baillie (London, 1910), especially pp. 217 ff., "The True Nature of Self-Certainty" and within this section pp. 228 ff., "Independence and dependence of self-consciousness: Lordship and Bondage". I base my interpretation, but without accepting his premisses, on Alexander Kojève's *Introduction à la Lecture de Hegel. Leçons sur la Phénoménologie de L'Esprit*, especially his commentary on the above section of Hegel's book, p. 11. See also my essays, *Hegel: Grösse und Grenzen* (Stuttgart, 1971).

object of this certainty. But recognition by other men does not take place without an external stimulus. It occurs only when the other person has himself first experienced the certainty of his own humanity (intelligence, superiority over nature).

Thus there are three separate strands which have to come together in order to produce the certainty of truth. These are, firstly, inner certainty, secondly, the act by which the object of this certainty is expressed in visible form, and, thirdly, the recognition of the one who acts and of his conscience by a fellow man.

Hegel's argument, as we know, concerns the dialectics of "lordship and bondage" through which the true nature of self-certainty becomes evident. The man who is courageous to the point of death has become superior to nature and has made himself lord, proves the rightness of his inner certainty by his outward acts and is thus recognized by his fellow man, who thereby turns himself into a bondsman or slave. But the recognition of the free, independent lord by the unfree, dependent slave who lives his life in chains, is ultimately of no value to the lord. He cannot attain to the true nature of self-certainty while the slave remains a slave. Only the slave who is made free and equal can help him to the realization of the true nature of his own self-certainty or make him truly free.

The slave, on the other hand, obtains the necessary "certainty" of his freedom by way of work. In his work he shows himself, in practice, to be as superior to nature as his master who has risked his natural life by throwing himself courageously into the battle.

The man who goes courageously to his death for the sake of an inner certainty (the certainty of faith) is known in the Christian tradition as a martyr. He is a man who bears witness outwardly to his inner certainty, and others know and recognize this inner certainty as truth because of his action of bearing witness to the point of death. Just as the martyr transcends the attitude of the lord, so the saint shows himself superior to the slave. The saint witnesses by his outward behaviour (moral acts, absolute personal self-surrender) to his inner certainty regarding faith and morals. The slave, on the other hand, shows, by his work, the dependence of outward nature (and his superiority over his own sensual desires).

The martyr is courageous to the point of death, like the lord, but he does not fight. The saint is superior to nature, like the slave, but he does not confine himself to working with nature. The lord and the slave are the prototypes from which Hegel developed his idea of the state and society. And in the same way, one can see the martyr and the saint as prototypes of the Church, although it is not my task here to work out a Hegelian ecclesiology.[2]

II. The Individual and Social Conscience

Whereas the Greek city states and the Roman Republic demanded the total subjection of the individual, and "freedom of conscience" could only appear as a factor in the dissolution of moral society as a whole, modern Christian society is familiar, at least in principle, with the rights of free conscience and the respect that must be accorded to the personal moral judgments of the individual.

But how can men live peacefully together when there are no rules which bind every individual? How can even intersubjective communication between individuals take place where there are no universally binding norms? How are such rules and norms to be constructed without destroying or limiting the individual's personal freedom?

To put the question in this way, however, is to misunderstand the nature of man. Humanly speaking, the individual exists only as the product of a human society existing before and at the same time as himself. The individual is always the product of a society. It is quite wrong to think of the individual as a complete and independent being who has subsequently to be reconciled with or be made part of society.

The individual lives from the beginning in a social environment previously created by society and can only live in that environment. Many rules and norms (like language, customs or moral laws) thus necessarily and spontaneously grow out of the development of the social individual. There is no other kind of individual and human life divorced from society does not exist. Even the solitary life only exists by virtue of its relationship with

---

[2] See especially the writings of Peter Gaston Fessard, s.j., on this subject.

society, whether past, present or future. There is therefore also no human existence without the objectively valid and accepted norms of society which are handed down to new generations as part of the human heritage. Some rules and norms have an absolute validity in every society and at every stage of history. We know that there are certain primitive tribes whose taboos have obtained so powerful a hold over the individual's mind that men die when the taboos are infringed.

Only at a certain level of social development does the individual free himself (in practice and in his mind) from the society that nurtures and conditions him and perhaps even come to some extent to oppose it. When this happens man acquires, for the first time, the inner experience of conscience working in opposition to the impulses of the individual.[3]

This contradiction was present earlier too, of course, but was concealed by the customs, rites and taboos that overlaid the person's natural impulses. If this contradiction did not exist, then it would not be possible to infringe taboos and experiences such as "guilt" would not exist.

For our present purpose, it is not necessary to establish the exact moment when collective self-consciousness gave way to individual self-consciousness in the West. This had certainly already occurred in later antiquity when Christianity was beginning to spread. The individual's conscience was often at odds not only with his own instinctive impulses, but also with the demands of an enclosed society and its leaders. In so far as the conscience was morally enlightened and purified, it tended in the direction of moral demands applicable to all men everywhere. The moral philosophy of the Stoics, for example, moved in the direction of world citizenship and humanitarianism.

[3] This freeing of the individual from the collective must be thought of in connection with the development of independent economic units (peasants or families with manual skills) who met each other only by way of trading in the market place. But it is surely wrong to assume that this new freedom and independence of families, and later of individuals, could one day, in the course of historical development, be reversed. Every development in history that leads to a new stage from which the previous stage can be grasped in theory and transcended in practice must be accepted as progress. But from the standpoint of the individual who has achieved independence the collective mentality cannot be understood as springing from the autonomous individual.

Ideally, the voice of conscience belongs to a universal society of all human beings, and even includes non-human elements such as animals and plants, either directly or indirectly, as necessary adjuncts to human life.[4]

The dignity and respect granted to the voice of conscience is due to its unique relationship with the world. Formally, the conscience, because of its total interiority, is granted special consideration as an example of moral freedom. When, for example, man's freedom of conscience is respected in constitutional law, this is because it is not possible to go behind the individual conscience, and because all moral acts are only moral in so far as they come from the conscience. Even when the government, in its legislation, comes to a different conclusion from that of the individual listening to his conscience (for example, when the law imposes military service), it is prepared to respect conscientious objections.

This attitude recognizes at the same time the possibility of error on both sides. The state recognizes its own fallibility by its respect for the individual conscience. But the individual conscience must also be recognized as fallible if it is not to be set up in an unjustifiable arrogance against the conscience of the government in its legislation.

But with the new formation of conscience and the necessity of recognizing its fallibility, there arises a new problem. Society and the state can protect themselves from "erroneous consciences"

[4] With the development of conscience, the individual frees himself, at least partially, from the conditions that supported him originally (the race, family, tribe or nation) and becomes, morally speaking, "autonomous". But this autonomy is moral only in so far as it is linked to the world-wide community of all men. This may not of course be true of all historically conditioned manifestations of man's conscience, but it seems to have been present from the beginning as a tendency.

This is not the place to speculate about the historical and theological relationship between the conscience and the universal Church, however close we may be to this subject. What is clear, however, is the simultaneous appearance of a universal conscience and, by its own claims, the institution of a universal Church, even though the Roman Empire may have been a secular example of the latter. But whereas the Roman Empire used its many gods for political purposes only—the political cult of the one state—the Church was concerned with the one universal God of revelation, who was not content with purely outward recognition, but demanded recognition in faith by man's conscience.

by *not* recognizing at least certain conscientious decisions and their consequences and forbidding any actions resulting from them under threat of penalties. These are generally actions which cannot be acceptable to the Christian conscience, for example, the private killing of a criminal. But in exceptional cases they may also be actions arising out of a Christian conscience, for example, the killing of a tyrant, which could be a moral obligation.

If we wish to prevent the individual conscience from claiming absolute rights, not merely in principle but in practice, then we must postulate an "objective" institution, recognizable and recognized, outside self-consciousness, which is to be the ultimate judge. The voice of conscience is absolute, but the information of the conscience can certainly err in individual instances. To be more precise, the voice of conscience is fallible in practice.

It is possible, of course, to postulate the existence of moral genius (or holiness), where fallibility does not arise, but this is an exception, not the rule. If we are to lessen the risks of erroneous decisions of conscience, then we require moral education, teaching and guidance. It is true that such education, teaching and guidance can only be provided by individuals who are themselves capable of acting erroneously. So we must postulate an institution that excludes the risk of human error. In Catholic teaching, this is the Church.[5]

From a purely scientific and anthropological standpoint, one can do no more than merely indicate the desirability and usefulness of such an institution. One cannot assert its reality. There is, however, in my opinion, an important exception to this general rule in the figure of the saint, who points to the historical evolution of infallible and absolutely binding rules of conduct and faith.

[5] By referring this institution back to divine foundation, which alone can safeguard from all error, we are explicitly underlining the proneness to error of *all* human institutions and organizations. This is the standpoint from which we condemn most sharply every kind of political absolutism, every suppression of minorities in the name of the state's wellbeing (as interpreted by a powerful minority). The unavoidable risk of error in all human institutions obliges these to be tolerant of criticism and legal opposition. The infallibility of the Church's pronouncements can never guarantee that any individual in the world will be free from error or "infallible".

III. Infallibility and the Church's Teaching Office

According to Catholic teaching, the Church guarantees Christian faith and the moral life based on that faith. The pronouncements of the Church—in councils and synods of bishops in agreement with the Pope or by the Pope when he speaks *ex cathedra*—are regarded as infallible. The possibility of this freedom from error cannot be scientifically demonstrated, but it can be shown to correspond with the moral need for guidance of individuals who are in the course of freeing themselves from the collective.

Christian faith is related to moral attitudes and behaviour, and is visibly expressed in both. Articles of faith that cannot be put into practice, even if only a question of man's attitude towards the Creator which is at the same time an attitude towards his creation, are meaningless. We must therefore assume that the Church believes its pronouncements in matters of faith to have decisive moral consequences for the individual and for society.

But the traditional Christian articles of faith are necessarily linked to an historically conditioned world of language and images that presuppose a different view of the world and of men. It is often difficult to distinguish (and can only afterwards be determined) where the real affirmation of faith ends and where the historically conditioned "form" of the pronouncement, the language used and the world-view implied, all the elements requiring alteration, begins.[6] Thus, for hundreds of years, Christian teaching was so closely linked to the Ptolemaic world-view that churchmen came to believe that this world-view was itself part of divine truth and had therefore to be defended against the newer cosmological discoveries.

The Soviet dialectical materialists of the present century have, of course, had a similar experience in condemning Einstein's relativity theory, Heisenberg's uncertainty principle and modern genetics because they were unable to reconcile these with certain

[6] Bultmann has attempted to extract the timeless content of faith from the statements of the evangelists and ultimately all that any theologian is doing is trying to translate from the language of the past into that of the present. There is no timeless language for timeless truth.

statements in their own philosophy.[7] But they later found that it was not absolutely necessary to reject these scientific theories, hypotheses or attempted explanations, in defence of the basic principles of dialectical materialism.

This philosophy is itself not really necessary for the establishment and development of the social and political system of socialism. Indeed its basic principles make far fewer demands—all that is required is the common ownership of the means of production, the universal obligation of work, and the insistence on equality, that is, the principle of equal pay for equal work. All this illustrates the tendency on the part of certain societies (like the Soviet Union or the Christian community) to make certain statements or pronouncements say more than what is required of them.

Just as man's understanding of the world has altered with the growth of the natural sciences and technology, so has the historically conditioned political and social order. We know that the Church has tried to accommodate itself to these changing conditions, though usually not without a struggle. It is true, however, that the usual motivation of the Church leaders has been the need to safeguard themselves and their people. Again and again, the Church deliberately placed itself on the side of tradition, and has continued to cling to this option even in face of revolutionary changes in society.

We think, for example, of the prohibition of usury in the Middle Ages, which was unable to prevent the development of a capitalist system, in which the Church eventually played its part.[8] Another example is the struggle against democracy in which the Catholic parties engaged for a long time in the nine-

---

[7] Cf. A. Buchholz, *Ideologie und Forschung in der sowjetischen Naturwissenschaft* (Stuttgart, 1953); S. Müller-Markus, *Einstein und die Sowjetphilosophie*, I (Dordrecht, 1960). On the other hand, in G. Klaus' and M. Buhr's philosophical dictionary, *Philosophisches Wörterbuch* (Berlin, 1970), the relativity theory is given positive recognition, and the "cosmological conclusions" (which were widely rejected by apologists of "Diamat" (dialectical materialism) up to 1956 are referred to as follows: "The cosmological conclusions drawn from the relativity theory are at present purely hypothetical. Whether we are part of a finite or infinite universe is also subject to the same presuppositions (e.g., cosmological principle or hierarchical structure)", *op. cit.*, p. 937.

[8] This useless struggle cannot simply be explained away as an "error". We must understand that it was the result of recognizing the morally

teenth century with Rome's approval. Whereas the primitive Church favoured the common ownership of possessions among the Christian communities, papal pronouncements during the last century defended private property with early bourgeois arguments, even when the requirement of "by one's own work" had long since been transcended.

Whenever the Church's pronouncements on faith and morals have to do with the contemporary understanding of the world, as, for example, in the case of Galileo, or with the current social or political order, they will necessarily lose their infallible character. They then become pronouncements of certain sectional groups and interests in exactly the same way as the statements of any overtly political party. But being *in* history and not above it, the Church is inevitably drawn into such sectional arguments and is thus faced with a dilemma. The Church has either to renounce all claims to infallibility because of this historically conditioned proneness to error, with a consequent weakening of effectiveness in its pronouncements, or to continue (without perhaps wanting it) to make infallible claims not only for its pronouncements on faith and morals, but also in the field of politics and sociology. I should like to conclude by suggesting a possible way out of this dilemma.

1. An increasing critical examination by the Church (in council, by popes, etc.) of the relevance of these pronouncements to political and social questions. This would certainly not make it possible to isolate all human error, but it would considerably reduce this risk. By critically examining its own statements for any suspicion of ideological content, the Church would to some extent exclude all ideologies, as Karl Mannheim in his later work has suggested with regard to secular matters.[9]

---

negative consequences of the new economic order. The Marxist explanation of the Church's impotence in opposing usury points primarily to the greater economic efficiency of the new capitalist system in comparison with the old feudal methods of production. Karl Marx could both condemn the capitalist system on moral grounds and justify it on historical grounds, because he anticipated its inevitable defeat. This view was not possible at the time of the Church's prohibition of usury and contradicts the Christian attitude.

[9] See especially Karl Mannheim, *Ideologie und Utopie* (Frankfurt, 3rd edn., 1952), p. 259: "The impulse to know society can be so directed that it will not make our being bound to our insights absolute. On the con-

2. The Church could—in all prudence—attempt to test the moral quality of the various social and political parties at odds with one another, and then support, with reservation, the party that seemed to give the best guarantee of increasing the number of those who can "afford" to follow their conscience freely and live a moral life. Such activity could not be classed as "infallible", but it would be good if the Church were able to engage in it.

3. The Church could try to take history more seriously—in the past, Catholic thought has been dominated too much by Aristotelian Thomism. The Church might also perhaps learn to accept the fact that, although pronouncements may have been free from error when they were made, they cannot be absolutely valid for all time.

Translated by Erika Young

The Concept of Infallibility

Patrick McGrath

THERE have been two notable attempts to show that the concept of infallibility, as traditionally understood, is not susceptible to rational employment in theology. In his book *Infallible? An Enquiry*, Hans Küng has argued on the basis of an examination of language that the traditional concept is incoherent. Language, he claims, is of its very nature an inadequate expression of reality. Every propositional statement is "subject to ambiguity, distortion, misunderstanding and error"[1].

To speak of a proposition as infallible is like speaking of a

---

trary, our discovery of the fact that we are bound in this way may make it possible for us to free ourselves initially from being bound. By adding my view to a view that is regarded as absolute, I neutralize the special quality of that view."
[1] Hans Küng, *Infallible? An Enquiry* (London, 1971), p. 139.

square that is circular, for "every proposition can be both true and false, depending on its aim, circumstances, meaning".[2] But if there can be no infallible propositions, then there can be no authority which is infallible in the traditional sense, for the only way in which such an authority could exercise its infallibility would be by uttering propositions which are infallible.

What Küng's argument amounts to, therefore, is that the traditional doctrine of infallibility must be rejected *a priori*; it is false not just as a matter of fact but as a matter of principle, for the concept of infallibility which it employs makes no sense. This argument is in my opinion unsound. It contains two defects, either of which is sufficient to invalidate it. None the less it raises several important points about the concept of infallibility and an examination of it should shed some light on the topic under discussion.

The first thing wrong with the argument is that it fails to distinguish between a propositional formula and a proposition. The concept of a proposition is not an easy one to define and philosophers are in some disagreement about it, but one thing seems undeniable—that a proposition is not to be identified with the propositional formula or set of symbols which is used to express it. This is clear from the fact that different propositional formulae can express the same proposition—e.g., "Two plus two equals four" and "$2+2=4$"—while the same propositional formula can express two or more different expressions—e.g., the oracle's advice to Pyrrhus: "Aio te, Aeacida, Romanos vincere posse".

Now the crucial part of Küng's critique of language—the part on which the validity of his argument depends—makes sense only if it is understood to refer not to propositions, but to propositional formulae. Thus when he writes that "every proposition can be both true or false, depending on its aim, circumstances, meaning", this is not merely true but platitudinous when understood of propositional formulae, but it is false if understood of propositions themselves. For example, the expression "The sun shining" expresses a false proposition as I write, but it expressed a true proposition yesterday. But this does not mean that a true proposition has become false, for it will always remain true that the sun was shining on the day in question. What has happened is that a propositional formula which yesterday expressed a true proposition now expresses a different proposition which is in fact false. The proposition which it expressed yesterday is still true, but one now requires a different propositional formula to express it. Equally when Küng writes, "A previous study of mine on the problem of Church definitions went beyond the statement made above that propositions can be true or false and concluded that they can be true and false",[3] what he is saying is true of propositional formulae, but false of propositions. Thus the expression "Queen Elizabeth never married" is true when understood of Elizabeth I, but false when understood of Elizabeth II. But this means not that the same proposition is true and false, but that the same propositional formula expresses two different propositions, one of which is true, the other false.

Küng is, of course, correct in thinking that every proposition which is genuinely informative and not a mere tautology is capable of being either true or false. But this in no way implies that the traditional concept of infallibility is incoherent. For the possibility of a proposition being false remains only so long as its truth has not been established. What the Vatican I definition claims is that a proposition, when asserted in certain circumstances by the Pope, is thereby guaranteed to be true so that its being false is no longer a real possibility. Küng's account of the limitations of language makes clear how easily such propositions may be misunderstood, but it does nothing to show that the Vatican I claim concerning them must be rejected as a matter of principle.

The second defect in Küng's argument is doctrinal rather than linguistic, and may be illustrated by the following quotation from his book: "Both supporters and opponents (of the Vatican I definition), the majority and the minority, assumed that the promises given to the Church were related to infallible propositions . . . they all without exception assumed that the promises given to the Church depended on infallible propositions."[4]

Here again Küng has overlooked a crucial distinction. It is one thing to assume that the infallibility of the Church can only be exercised in the assertion of propositions; it is quite a different thing to assume that such propositions are infallible. The Fathers at Vatican I made the first assumption, but not the second. The

[3] *Op. cit.*, p. 140.   [4] *Op. cit.*, pp. 124-5.

Vatican I definition says nothing about infallible statements or propositions. It ascribes infallibility to the Pope and Church alone. Of the solemn definitions of the Pope and the Church it says, not that they are infallible, but that they are irreformable, that the Church cannot subsequently revoke them. Infallibility and irreformability are clearly different characteristics. Infallibility is necessarily connected with truth and falsity, irreformability is not. A law could be irreformable (the divine law presumably is) but it would make no sense to speak of a law as infallible. Hence in stating that the Pope and Church can speak infallibly in certain circumstances, the Vatican Council was not maintaining that what they said on those occasions consisted of infallible propositions.

But could one not argue that this follows as a matter of course from the Vatican definition, since Pope or Church could not be said to speak infallibly if the propositions they assert were not infallible? This position seems plausible at first glance, but I believe that we have only to consider it briefly to realize that it is untenable. Modern linguistic philosophy has familiarized us with the idea that in discussing highly abstract problems such as those of philosophy and theology, we may utter remarks which, while impeccable from the point of view of grammar and syntax, turn out on examination to be devoid of sense. One way in which this may happen is when we commit what Gilbert Ryle calls a "category mistake", that is when we allocate a concept to a logical category to which it does not belong. If we were to describe a sound by means of a colour concept—"a yellow scream"—and intend our remark to be taken literally, then we would be guilty of a mistake of this kind. A rather more endearing example is contained in the story about the African colony where, shortly before independence was granted, people came to the local missionary and inquired anxiously whether independence would be delivered to them by a government official or whether they would be able to collect it at the bank. More sophisticated examples may be found in the writings of philosophers and theologians. Thus Bernard Lonergan in his book *Insight* frequently mentions "acts of knowing" and "acts of understanding". The logical impropriety of these modes of expression becomes clear when we consider the remarks, "I was understanding when you came into the room" or "I was knowing when the ball rang". If knowing and understanding belonged to the category of actions, these would be perfectly intelligible utterances, whereas in fact it is impossible to attach any sense to them.

Now to speak of infallible propositions is to commit, it seems to me, that sort of category mistake. Infallible propositions are impossible not in the way in which it is impossible for water to freeze at 10° or to boil at 90°, but in the way in which it is impossible for screams to be yellow or for independence to be obtained over the counter. The impossibility is logical rather than factual. Only a person can err in the sense of accepting a proposition as true when in fact it is false. And therefore only a person or a community of persons such as the Church can enjoy immunity from error of this kind. We say that a proposition is erroneous or incorrect or false, but we never say that it errs, for to err is to do something that only a person or something akin to a person can do.

But what if a proposition were free from the possibility, not of erring, but of being erroneous? Would this not enable one to ascribe infallibility to it? The answer is no, because there would then be no intrinsic difference between an infallible proposition and a merely true one. A proposition which is true cannot possibly be false any more that an even number cannot possibly be uneven; in each case you are dealing with mutually exclusive characteristics. Hence if an infallible proposition is one which cannot be false, "infallible" is merely a misleading synonym for "true"; and this cannot be what is meant by those who claim that the power of enunciating such propositions is a supernatural gift which was bestowed on the Church by Christ. The ability to assert true propositions may not be the most obvious of human characteristics, but not even in the case of higher ecclesiastics would one be tempted to regard it as a supernatural gift.

A persistent opponent may still argue, however, that the difference between an infallible proposition and a true one is that the impossibility of being false is only conditional for a true proposition, but it is absolute for an infallible one. A proposition that one believes to be true may always turn out to be false, for the belief that it is true may be incorrect. And this means that the impossibility of the proposition being false is never absolute but always dependent on its being genuinely true and not merely believed to be such. An infallible proposition, on the other hand, simply cannot be false; the infallible judgment of the Pope or Church is sufficient to ensure this.

This, I am afraid, is an attempt to create a distinction where none exists. For the impossibility of an infallible proposition being false is itself dependent on the authority which declares it being genuinely infallible and not merely thought to be such. And the belief that this authority is infallible cannot itself be justified by reference to the declaration of an infallible authority without involving oneself in a vicious circle or an infinite regress. The truth of an "infallible proposition" is therefore dependent on the truth of another proposition which is not itself "infallible". Hence the impossibility of being false is no more absolute for an "infallible proposition" than for a proposition which is true but not "infallible".

Before ending this section it might be added that while the phrase an "infallible proposition", if interpreted strictly, involves a category mistake, it is often used as a convenient shorthand for "a proposition which has been infallibly declared to be true by the Pope or the Church"; and of course it then involves no logical impropriety. But the point is that if we use the term "infallible proposition" in our explanation of the doctrine of infallibility, we are in danger of thinking that infallible propositions constitute a class of super-propositions which differ intrinsically from non-infallible ones; and hence that a separate question arises about their possibility. But this, as we have seen, is a false problem. If the concept of infallibility is incoherent, it is not because propositions cannot be infallible.

II

The second attempt to show the impossibility of any rational use of the concept of infallibility in theology was made by the Church of Ireland divine, George Salmon, in his book *The Infallibility of the Church*. Despite its age and faded scholarship this is still the most acute critique of the Vatican I teaching on infallibility, though this is perhaps less a commendation of

Salmon than a reflection on his rivals. Salmon's aim is less radical than Küng's. What he seeks to show is not that the concept of infallibility is incoherent, but that one cannot have an adequate reason for believing any doctrine which employs it. His argument may be summarized as follows: Catholics accept the infallibility of the Church because they believe that without an infallible teacher there can be no certainty on matters of revealed religion. Now infallibility will provide certainty only if the doctrine of infallibility is itself certain. But its certainty cannot be based on the infallibility of the Church without involving oneself in a vicious circle and it cannot be based on something else without admitting that certainty can, after all, be reached on matters of revealed religion without recourse to infallibility. Hence a Catholic can never have an inadequate reason for believing the doctrine of infallibility to be true.

A man may say "I am absolutely certain that I am right in my religious opinions, because I believe what the Pope believes, and he is absolutely certain not to believe wrong". But then comes the question, "How come you to be absolutely certain that the Pope is absolutely certain not to believe wrong?" It is not possible to answer this question without being guilty of the logical fallacy of arguing in a circle.[5]

This argument, like Küng's, will not stand up to serious examination. All that Salmon has succeeded in showing is that a Catholic who believes that without infallibility there can be no certainty cannot provide a reason for believing in the Church's infallibility without being guilty of either inconsistency or of the fallacy of arguing in a circle. He has given us no reason for thinking that belief in infallibility of necessity involves the belief that without infallibility there can be no certainty concerning revelation. If these two beliefs are logically independent of each other—and there seems to be no good reason for thinking that they are not—then arguments for infallibility cannot be ruled out *a priori* as logically invalid.

What *is* true, however, is that Catholics have often argued that

[5] George Salmon, *The Infallibility of the Church* (London, 1888), revised edition 1952, p. 21.

without recourse to infallibility there can be no certainty in matters of religion. Thus Bishop B. C. Butler has recently tried to establish the reality of the Church's infallibility by claiming that "if the Church's power to define infallibly is denied, then the Church is *unable* to proceed from understanding to unhesitating judgment, and revelation is not effectively transmitted".[6] This type of argument leaves one completely open to Salmon's attack. And what is equally true is that defenders of infallibility have a compelling motive for wanting to argue in this way. For if certainty is attainable without infallibility, then the Church does not absolutely need infallibility for carrying out of its mission—it may still be a useful aid, but it can no longer be regarded as an essential requirement. And this means that the case for the infallibility is enormously weakened. If the Church could not function properly without infallibility, then, granted its divine origin, it must have been endowed with it. But if infallibility is not an essential requirement, then the case for the Church's infallibility rests entirely on the far from unambiguous testimony of Scripture and tradition.

That defenders of infallibility have a compelling motive for arguing that infallibility is required for certainty is, however, a different thing from claiming that the doctrine of infallibility logically implies this; and unless the latter claim is true, Salmon's argument is unsound. In fact Salmon gives the game away himself when he considers Bishop Clifford's contention that the doctrine of infallibility is based, not on the infallible teaching of the Church, but on the testimony of Scripture. Having considered the weaknesses in Clifford's attempt to derive infallibility from Scripture, Salmon concludes, quite rightly, that infallibility cannot provide certainty if it is itself based on arguments whose validity is doubtful. But the point is that Clifford's argument has merely turned out on examination to be less than probative, whereas Salmon's original claim was that any such argument must of its very nature involve a logical fallacy. The fact that Salmon has to examine Clifford's argument to show that it is inadequate is enough to indicate that his original claim was unwarranted.

[6] B. C. Butler, "The Limits of Infallibility", *The Tablet*, vol. 225, p. 399.

III

Despite this Salmon's argument is of considerable significance and should not be dismissed by saying simply that it establishes nothing more than that defenders of infallibility are sometimes inconsistent. It draws attention to two significant facts about infallibility. The first is that infallibility is of no value for the attainment of certainty unless it is itself certain. The second is that defenders of infallibility tend to put forward circular arguments in its support. A further examination of these points must, I fear, raise serious doubts about the usefulness of the concept of infallibility in explaining the nature of the Church's teaching authority.

An appeal to the infallible teaching of the Church will provide certainty on matters of doctrine only if one is already certain that the Church is infallible. And this latter certainty, as Salmon has pointed out, cannot itself be based on infallibility without involving oneself in a vicious circle; it must therefore be based on other grounds. Now the certainty on which infallibility depends goes well beyond infallibility itself. To be certain that the Church is infallible one must be certain that Christ was a divine emissary, that he founded a Church, that he set up a teaching authority within it, that he had the power to endow this authority with the gift of infallibility and that he did in fact do so. Since the Church could not be infallible unless all these things were true, it follows that certainty concerning their truth cannot be based on the infallibility of the Church.

This places a considerable restriction on the scope of infallibility; it means that it has no power to provide certainty in a whole area of doctrine which includes some of the most important and basic elements of Christian belief. Furthermore, even within the area of doctrine where it can function, the exercise of infallibility does not produce certainty, but rather presupposes it. For the defining authority must first be certain that the doctrine has been genuinely revealed before it can define it. To suppose otherwise is to conjure up the extraordinary hypothesis of a Pope or Council defining a doctrine and imposing it on the faithful without themselves being certain beforehand that it had been revealed. It follows that a claim, such as Bishop Butler's, that without infallibility certainty is impossible is not merely not true of Christian doctrine in general; it isn't even true of any particular aspect of it. Certainty about doctrine is a presupposition of the exercise of infallibility rather than a consequence of it.

Nevertheless, infallibility could still carry out the more modest role of providing believers with an assurance that much of what the Church solemnly proclaims is true. It can do this, however, only if the evidence for infallibility itself warrants certainty, since an assertion of infallibility which is itself uncertain obviously cannot provide certainty on other matters of doctrine. It does not fall within the scope of this article to evaluate the evidence for the infallibility of the Church, but one thing seems evident— if Christ did endow the Church with infallibility, he would surely have made it abundantly clear that he had done so. The whole point of infallibility is to provide a secure means of ending doubt on matters of doctrine. And this it cannot do if the presence of infallibility is itself doubtful. For Christ to grant infallibility to the Church in a merely implicit way—and arguments for infalli-bility often suggest this—would be equivalent to giving some-thing with one hand while taking it back with the other. It would be to endow the Church with the means to put an end to doubt on matters of doctrine, but in such a way that the means can never function effectively. The question to be asked about the doctrine of infallibility, therefore, is not simply whether there is evidence to support it, but whether the evidence is any-where near as clear-cut as the character of the doctrine itself demands. In this instance inadequate evidence is hardly better than no evidence at all. And one cannot help asking: If the evi-dence is so convincing, why has the doctrine been so contro-versial?

The second significant point which emerged from Salmon's critique of infallibility was the danger of putting forward cir-cular arguments in its support. Salmon believed that any argu-ment in favour of infallibility must inevitably be circular in char-acter. This claim, as we have seen, cannot be sustained, but it is not entirely unwarranted. For a defender of infallibility will almost inevitably fall back on the authority of the Church to bolster up his argument if he finds that on its own it is incapable of providing certainty. However, this inevitability is not logical, for there is no *a priori* reason why arguments for infallibility must be inadequate. If they are so in fact, then this is a contingent matter, which could have been otherwise.

A much greater danger of circularity occurs when one considers the conditions which must govern the exercise of infallibility. Here there is the same need for certainty as there is concerning the presence of infallibility in the Church. Infallibility will provide certainty only if one is already certain, not merely that the Church is infallible, but also as to where one finds the infallible voice of the Church. To say that the Church is infallible is to say very little until one has answered the questions: Who in the Church is infallible? In what circumstances? Concerning what subject-matter? Each of these questions can be answered only by answering a series of sub-questions which generate their own difficulties. Take the first, for instance. It is commonly held that a General Council is one of the infallible voices of the Church. But who has the power to convoke a General Council? Who decides its membership and on what principles? Must it be genuinely representative of the Church as a whole and could it be such if the laity, not to mention ordinary clergy, are excluded from any active role in it? Even if it is representative of the Church of its time, how far, if at all, can a Council held at one period be held to represent the Church of another period? How are decisions on doctrinal matters to be arrived at—by simple majority, moral unanimity or something in between? (A very real question in view of the eccentric way in which membership of General Councils was proportioned between different areas in the Church; at Vatican I, for instance, almost thirty per cent of the bishops present were from Italy.) Most important of all, who is to answer these questions and how can we tell if the answers are correct? Unless they can be answered with certainty, no exercise of infallibility by a General Council will provide certainty on a matter of doctrine.

One might say in reply that the answers come from the non-infallible teaching of the Church; the fact that the teaching is fallible does not mean that it is uncertain, while at the same time it rules out the danger of circularity in argument. But even if we overlook the other difficulties here—and this is to overlook a great deal—does this not deprive infallibility of any real meaning? What assurance can a claim to infallibility give if the validity of the claim is dependent on a whole series of propositions whose truth is not vouched for by infallibility? The conclusion of an argument cannot be more certain than the premisses on which it depends. So what is to be gained by calling a doctrine infallible if its infallibility is so dependent on the non-infallible teaching of the Church? In any event if the non-infallible teaching of the Church can provide certainty on so many difficult matters, then what use is infallibility? It seems to provide no compensation for the many difficulties it creates.

The recent history of the Church would appear to confirm these considerations. Infallibility was not exercised by either the Second Vatican Council or by Pope Paul in his attempt to give a definitive answer to the problem of birth-control. Yet would anyone claim that the authority of the Council's teaching was thereby lessened or that the birth-control controversy would have ended if *Humanae Vitae* had been infallibly proclaimed? Or does anyone seriously think that the difficulties which beset the believer today on matters of faith could be removed by a series of papal or conciliar definitions? Fallible man cannot be provided with an absolute assurance against error. The pilgrim Church has indeed been assured that it will reach its goal; but this does not mean that any particular step is in the right direction.

III. The Problem of the Infallibility of the Church's Office

A Theological Reflection

Edward Schillebeeckx

I. Man's Answer in Faith belongs to the Content of Revelation

IF IT is true that an historical event can be so decisive that it
has to be expressed in the language of faith, then this speaking
about God's activity in history can only be meaningful if man's
interpretative understanding of this in faith belongs to revelation
itself. Revelation and man's interpretative understanding of
revelation in faith are correlative. An historical event cannot be
recognized as a decisive act of God unless it is understood and
accepted on the basis of a definite experience as *de facto* determinative for our understanding of ourselves and of the whole of
reality and especially of our life in practice. This is the meaning
of the rather vague formula "Jesus is Lord". The Christian reply
to any question about the determinative factor in their lives is to
point to Jesus of Nazareth, confessed as the Christ, the only-be-
gotten Son.

Revelation, then, is God's saving activity in history experienced and expressed by believers in answer to the question about
the meaning of life. It is a reduction to call the mere fact of
God's activity revelation in itself, without interpretation, or to
call this interpretation as such revelation, in which case faith
would be no more than a subjective view of history. Revelation
includes both these aspects and, because it is only fulfilled *in*
man's response, it can never be discussed in a completely objective, scientific or historically critical way.

In its aspect of knowing, faith is, moreover, an interpretative knowledge; in other words, theology as interpretation is not only valid as a reflection about faith and its content, but is also valid *in* the content of faith itself, as expressed, and *in* revelation itself, also as expressed. This interpretative—in other words, theological —aspect of the reply given by believers belongs essentially to the *content* of revelation and of faith and dogma, both in the case of the central content of faith and in that of the peripheral aspects of faith graded according to a "hierarchy of truths",[1] and not simply to the way in which revelation and faith are expressed. The whole of revelation and of faith and dogma are *in* history. There is no zone that is immune from the storms of man's history, no zone of pure theology. God's saving activity is only formal revelation so long as it is expressed in faith, on the basis of living experience, by men who are *in* history. This makes it more difficult for us to speak about an identity of Christian faith, because that identity is so interwoven with man's history, his redemption and his integrity.

II. THE PROMISE OF GOD'S HELP

In itself, the Church is not able to remain faithful to this identity in an historical event, but is, as the product of men who want good but often do evil, ambiguous. The Church's faith and proclamation of that faith will not, however, cease, according to the promise expressed in the gospel of Matthew, which begins with the confession of Emmanuel, God with us (Matt. 1. 23) and ends with Emmanuel, God with us in Jesus Christ: "I am with you always, to the close of the age" (Matt. 28. 20).

The structure of the ancient covenant was basically "I shall be with you—you will be with me", yet, despite the difference between and the deep continuity of the Old and the New Testaments, the promise of this covenant is not an automatic or purely juridical guarantee of success.

In the first draft of the Constitution on the Church, the biblical mystery of the "community of the Christ" was identified simply with the Catholic Church, but in the definitive text the wording is more sensitive and finely shaded: "Haec ecclesia . . . *subsistit in* ecclesia catholica".[2] This "subsists in", meaning "is present in a

---

[1] Decree *Unitatis redintegratio* on Ecumenism, 11.
[2] Constitution *Lumen gentium* on the Church, 8.

veiled form", does not have any specifically scholastic significance. On the contrary, it is clear from the *acta* of the Council
that the words were deliberately chosen in order to dilute the
first and stronger expression of the Church's exclusive identity:
"Haec ecclesia . . . *est* ecclesia catholica".[3] The commission com-
mented: "This empirical Church reveals the mystery (of the
Church), but not without shadows . . . although this lack of lustre
does not make the manifestation of the mystery completely impossible" (*op. cit.*). The manifestation of the Church thus becomes manifest—or recognizable—*in* the Catholic Church "in
sin and in purification".[4] Weakness and sin can only be overcome
"by the power of Christ and by love" (*op. cit.*), so that it may
be said that this Church is called to be "sancta simul et puri-
ficanda"—"at the same time holy and always in need of being
purified".[5]

This applies to the whole Church—there is no part of its concrete life where this is not so. The Church's "remaining in the
truth" and remaining perfectly faithful is made possible by the
promise and the call "never to cease to renew herself".[6] Far from
being triumphant in this claim to "indefectibility", the Church
manifests a weakness in which only God's grace is triumphant.

This indefectibility is, moreover, not a static, "essential" characteristic of the Church, but something which involves the
Church's dynamic and existential faith in the promise. The truth
of revelation is a truth of witness, in which the bond between the
person and message is always present. The promise of indefectibility is made *interior* in the Church itself in and through faith,
hope and love which always urge the Christian to *metanoia* and
renewal. This promise is not merely juridical and without historical form. In the Constitution on the Church, this indefectibility is attributed to the constant activity of the Holy Spirit: "so
that . . . moved by the Holy Spirit, (the Church) may never cease
to renew herself".[7] The Holy Spirit, the *telos* or End of the
Trinity, brings, as a gift to the Church the Church itself to the
End.

---

[3] "Loco *est* dicitur *subsistit in*, ut expressio melius concordet cum
affirmatione de elementis ecclesialibus quae alibi adsunt" (*Relatio de
singulis numeris, Relatio* in n. 8, p. 25).

[4] *Op. cit.*, p. 23.   [5] *Lumen gentium*, 8.

[6] *Op. cit.*, 9.   [7] *Op. cit.*, 9.

All this is said of the Church as a whole, before any distinction is made between the community and its office-bearers; the promise applies to both. The indefectibility of the Church is faithfulness expressed in a history, not only of human attitudes, but also of grace itself, going before man, so that the Church, in its concrete historical form, is always limping behind it. The real history of the Church, then, is a history of constant decline and renewal. What can and what cannot be reformed are always so inextricably interwoven that the Church cannot always distinguish them. By virtue of grace, the Church is at the same time both *metanoia* and self-correction and subject both to the promise and to the New Testament warning, "judgment begins with the household of God" (1 Pet. 4. 17–18).

III. INDEFECTIBILITY OF OFFICE

After outlining the ecclesiological background to the problem, we must now turn to the concept of the infallibility of office as expressed in the papacy and the Church's councils. All the Christian denominations believe, after all, in God's promise of help to the "communities of God", that the message of the Gospel will never cease to be heard and that this lasting quality implies a "remaining in the truth".

These two aspects are inseparable—the "Church" that no longer "remains in the truth" is no longer a "community of God" or "of Christ". The context of the Matthaean logion, "I shall be with you", is Jesus' speaking about the "baptizing" and "teaching" Church (Matt. 28. 18–20). The promise is made to the Church's *confession* in both functions. It is hardly possible to accept, from the ecclesiological point of view, that the Church, in its confession of baptism, can "remain in the truth" if there is no promise that its teaching will have a similar lasting value. The Church's "remaining in the truth" implies faithfulness in the teaching Church.

The same "presence in a veiled form" (*subsistere in*) of the biblical mystery in the Roman Catholic Church applies not only to the community of God as a whole, but also to the Church's confession in the teaching of those holding office. There is, in other words, no simple identity between the dogmatic confession of faith and the Word of God. Before discussing what is meant by the dogma of infallibility, however, I should like to outline the context within which this pronouncement ought to be examined if its significance is to be properly understood and it is not to contradict all the concrete facts of human experience and thought.

1. *The Perspectivism of Every Assertion of Truth*

An assertion may be both true and untrue according to the sphere or context of questioning and understanding in which it is situated. This has been said often enough by linguistic analysts and, in a different context, by Hans Küng[8] and now Bernard Lonergan has written that the relativists make three basic premisses. The first is that the significance of every assertion is relative, that is, it is related to its context. The second is that every context is subject to change and is situated within a process of development and/or decline. Thirdly, it is not possible to predict what the context will be in the future.[9] He then goes on to say that these premisses are, as such, correct. It does not, for example, follow from the first premiss that the context cannot be replaced. Within the replaced context, a correct assertion is recognizably true and cannot at the same time be untrue. With regard to the second premiss, it may happen that an assertion which was true in its own context will be incorrect in a different context. The fact that it can be proved by an historical reconstruction of the original context that this assertion was true in that context means that we can recognize the truth that was originally intended.[10]

Truth can only be attained from an historically situated perspective—it is not itself "perspectivistic", but absolute, yet we can only possess it in an historical, perspectivistic or relative way. The historical sphere or context of questioning within which an assertion provides an answer also determines the truth of that assertion. The interpretative question is the real crux of the whole process of interpretation and of the answer or interpretative assertion, especially if interpretative knowledge is sought. The

[8] *Infallible? An Enquiry* (London, 1971).
[9] B. Lonergan, *Doctrinal Pluralism* (Milwaukee, 1971), p. 10.
[10] *Op. cit.*, pp. 10–11.

"hermeneutical situation", the situational context from which the interpreter questions what is to be interpreted, is historical and therefore variable. All these components of the "context" are concentrated in the questions that are asked of what has to be interpreted and this marks off the "sphere of understanding" or background to the interpretative question which guides the whole process of understanding.

G. Vass rightly insists that one aspect of every question is orientated towards the object, so that the situation within which it is asked has a fundamental significance with regard to the answer that will be given.[11] The question anticipates *possible* alternatives and the verifiable certainty of the preferred alternative. Without this orientation, it is meaningless or else impossible to ask an interpretative question. If the answer is already known, the question is unreal and a question cannot be asked unless possible alternatives are anticipated in it—this is a *necessary* condition for any search for truth. What is more, the possibility that there are sufficient reasons for one of the possible alternatives to be preferred as an answer must also be anticipated. In a word, what is contained within the norm of what is to be interpreted and within the framework of the questioning and its anticipations is "interpretative knowledge".

With regard to the truth of an interpretation, we are clearly wrong to call a conclusion true or false, thus paying attention *only* to the "answer in itself", that is, to the final assertion, without taking into consideration the questioning within its historical context. In *interpretative* knowledge, the ultimate assertion is only true or false within the context of questioning and understanding. In other words, the whole historical context of the questioning itself is an integral part of the whole interpretative truth. I would therefore agree here with Lévi-Strauss when he insisted that the wise man is not the man who gives true answers, but the man who asks the right questions.[12]

This is not a form of relativism, but a recognition that coming to the truth is a continuous historical process. It would un-

---

[11] G. Vass, "On the Historical Structure of Christian Truth", in *The Heythrop Journal*, 9 (1968), pp. 129–42, 274–89; Vass's answer to the question of truth is, in my opinion, insufficient.

[12] *Mythologica*, I (Paris, 1971), p. 19.

doubtedly lead to relativism if the problem of truth were regarded as finally settled, in which case truth would be the correct
answer to correct, historically determined questions and would
no longer have any universal significance. In that case, "true" is
what provides the most coherent answer to a contingent questioning. Truth is thus an inner coherence between question and
answer, on the one hand, a discovery of a certain historical situation which is expressed in a certain form of questioning as a
problem and, on the other, the most suitable answer given to
that questioning.[13] The ultimate answer to the question of truth
cannot be found in this correlation because truth is orientated towards a universal consensus. The correlation between a correct
question and a correct answer is not the universal truth towards
which man consciously tends, but man who lives in history cannot dispense with historical perspectivism.

This means that truth, which is always sought within a constantly changing situation of question and answer and a basically
historical contingency, is never found only in *my* interpretation
of reality, but only in my going beyond my own historical
answer. In other words, the historically situated answer is only
"true" in so far as it is included in a continuous historical process. Within the current of history, each human being has here
and now, that is, "perspectivistically", a place where he is in-
vited to ask a question that no one else can ask.[14] However historically determined my question and my answer may be, my
fundamental need is to say something that is valid here and
now and at the same time universal. It is, in other words, only
when my truth is played off against the other person's truth in
dialogue that we are really *on the way towards* the truth in history. Each man needs the other person's truth both of the past
and of the future in order to come to the fullness of truth; as
Paul Ricoeur has said, the truth is the *magnet* of our articulations. A true assertion is the result of our seizing hold of the
correct perspective of truth within an historically determined
situation of question and answer.

[13] P. Ricoeur, *Histoire et vérité* (Paris, 1955), p. 52.
[14] *Op. cit.*, pp. 54-5.

2. *The Perspectivism of the Articulations of Faith*

As I have already said, revelation is God's saving activity in human history experienced and expressed by the community of believers who interpret it. In that case, the Christian confession of faith comes within the category of interpretative knowledge and shares the historical nature of the situation of question and answer.

Dogmatic definitions have at times been put forward by the Church as an expression of authentic Christian faith, whereas at other times this literal articulation has been condemned by the same Church. A few examples of this may show how the historically determined situation of question and answer and man's seizing hold of the correct objective perspective which transcends that situation are both fundamental to the Church's definitions of faith. The early anti-Pelagian pronouncements can be contrasted with the Church's condemnation of the teaching of M. de Bay, Jansen and Quesnel to provide a good illustration of what I mean. Both in the early documents (the *Indiculus Pseudo-Caelestini*, DS 239, which is of doubtful dogmatic value, the Second Council of Orange, D 383, and the Synod of Quiercy, DS 622) and in the more recent texts (condemning the reformers and the Jansenists, DS 1515 and 1388), the Church's attitude towards the effect of sin on human freedom is made clear. In the first case, the Church declares that man's freedom is lost through (original) sin, whereas in the second case the false teachers are condemned for asserting that man's freedom is lost through (original) sin. The same articulation or statement thus expresses Christian faith in the first case and false teaching in the second. Other examples are the early and medieval Church's condemnation of the teaching that man could do good without grace (DS 240, 242, 243, 244; 379, 390, 392, 393, 395; 725) in contrast to the later Church's defence of this statement against de Bay and the Jansenists (DS 1927–1930; 1937, 1965, 2308, 2438–2442) and the early Church's defence of the assertion that sinners and unbelievers could only perform sinful actions (DS 392) as against the later condemnation of the same statement when it was made by the Jansenists (DS 1925, 1927, 1935, 1938, 1940; also Trent, 1557).

This problem can be solved if we bear in mind that the same

statement may be materially both true and false according to the historical context of question and answer within which it is placed. The early texts express a reaction against the Pelagian optimism of natural ethics, whereas the later assertions are a reaction against the pessimistic view of corrupt human freedom. What is more, a different understanding of freedom is reflected in each case. The early Church saw freedom as "freedom to good" and sinful action—in modern terminology, a free self-determination to evil—as an absence of freedom and slavery.[15] Later, however, the Church integrated Aristotle's anthropological concept into its earlier Augustinian view of freedom, so that what was correctly defended by the early Church was also correctly condemned by the later Church. The Augustinian approval and the Aristotelian disapproval do not formally apply to the same assertion, because both statements were made within different historical contexts of understanding. The same distinction applies to what is materially the same assertion that there cannot and that there can be ethically good actions without grace. The early Church had a specifically Christian view of ethical goodness as a human action measured against its saving aspect. The later Church, on the other hand, was aware of the anthropological aspect of the goodness of human activity.

Any scandal caused by such antithetic statements made by the Church can be overcome by bearing in mind that they were made in an historical situation of question and answer. In condemning Jansenism, however, did the Church sufficiently respect the Jansenists' Augustinian and therefore conservative context of questioning and understanding in the light of its new and so to speak progressive understanding? One of the chief causes of polarization in human communications is the existence of radically different spheres of understanding at one and the same period. The Jansenists can rightly be accused of "conservatism" in their strict adherence of the literal teaching of Augustine and the early Church and their blindness to the contemporary historical context. What we cannot, however, say *a priori* is that their assertions, situated within a context of understanding which

[15] In the Middle Ages, we find Thomas Aquinas accepting this Augustinian concept of freedom, but at the same time linking it with the Aristotelian concept; see *De veritate*, q. 22, a. 6.

had become antiquated, were *per se* incorrect precisely within that context. It is clear that some awareness of the reason for this mutual lack of understanding was present in the Church, since the general condemnation of Jansenist teaching was modified from "heretical" to "offensive to ordinary believers" (*offensiva piarum auriculorum*).

I have deliberately chosen examples of the Church's condemnation of "conservative" teaching, not because I wanted to contrast "conservatism" with "progressivism", but because I wanted to draw attention to the question of *creative faithfulness* to the Gospel, a faithfulness which is only possible in a changing and developing history. Furthermore, there is sufficient evidence in the life and practice of the Church to show that the same assertion may be both true and untrue according to the context of understanding and to semantic usage. The consequence of this is that it is not possible to speak in advance about the "irrevocable" character of certain pronouncements made by the Church's teaching office if the historical context of questioning and understanding and the changing semantic usage of language are disregarded. If the charism of infallibility is to be at all meaningful, it must have a special function within this context. What is more, it is not possible for the teaching Church to speak of "heterodoxy" without having previously examined its own context of questioning and understanding and without having ensured that it is not projecting its own questions into the mind of the author whose work is being examined. The teaching Church may, on the other hand, well have a pastoral duty to draw the attention of believers to the possibility of misunderstanding to which certain writings may give rise.

3. *A Legitimate or a Necessary Process?*

Another very important question has, however, to be answered before we can discuss the First Vatican Council's dogma of infallibility—is the interpretation that has been practised throughout the Church's history a *necessary* process, in view of the origins of the Christian Church, or is it simply a *legitimate* process, in view of the historical contingency of the questions?[16]

[16] This has been most clearly formulated as a *question* by M. Wiles in *The Making of Christian Doctrine* (Cambridge, 1967), pp. 1–17.

If our human affirmations of truth are conditioned by the historical situation of question and answer within which these affirmations are made, we must, on the basis of this historical contingency, consciously admit that our articulations of our knowledge of truth, in so far as they are true, are legitimate but not necessary. Dogma might, for instance, have developed along entirely different lines if the historical models of interpretation had been different. But, even within a "system immanent" development, new experiences exert pressure on earlier models, in which case we have to choose between two possibilities. We may leave the earlier model unchanged and try to let it absorb the new experiences. In this case, new "system immanent" difficulties, which can only be dealt with by applying very subtle distinctions, accumulate until the earlier model is broken open. The alternative is to replace this earlier model by a perhaps provisional model which will enable the new experiences to be better accommodated and understood.[17] This second model gives us the key by which legitimate differences between many of the interpretations of the Eastern churches and many of those of the Latin Church can be explained. "Remaining in the truth" is a concrete historical reality, not a supra-historical reality for the churches.

IV. INFALLIBILITY

The dogma of infallibility, as defined by the First Vatican Council, must now be considered within the historical context of question and answer if it is to be at all meaningful. It is clear from recent controversy that the term "infallibility" as applied to the Church's "remaining in the truth" is widely regarded as unsatisfactory. Many Catholics are uncertain as to the precise scope and meaning of the dogma itself and Walter Kasper has undoubtedly expressed, in the introduction to his critical defence of Hans Küng's argument, what many Catholics believe.[18] Other

[17] In this context, B. Welte has rightly spoken of a sensational change in man's thinking, of periodic cracks appearing in the mind of the Christian community; see H. Schlier and others, *Zur Frühgeschichte der Christologie* (Freiburg, 1970), pp. 100–17.
[18] W. Kasper, "Zur Diskussion um das Problem der Unfehlbarkeit", *Stimmen der Zeit*, 188 (1971), pp. 363–5.

Christians sometimes have the impression that Catholics have to "pretend" that papal infallibility is virtually all-embracing[19] and the Church has never officially protested against this very non-Catholic idea.

Infallibility as such is an attribute of truth; they have virtually the same meaning. Since the time of Descartes, the question has already been, however, how can we be *sure* that we are "in the truth"? In Christian terms, the question is whether "infallibility", as a form of the Church's "remaining in the truth" can be localized. All Christians confess the infallibility of the universal Church, but both Luther and Calvin restricted this to the Word of God, believing that the universal Church, as a "creature of the Word", could not err in its confession of faith, but at the same time that it was possible to verify jurisdictionally the Church's infallible pronouncements.[20] Most Protestants would insist that the concrete infallibility of Roman Catholic teaching cannot be verified, because God's promise is grace, not something at the "disposal" of any body such as the Church. The community of believers as a whole is infallible in its confession of faith, but the presence of the Church's "remaining in the truth" can never be guaranteed—it surprises us by its presence. It is only in Scripture that there is, according to the reformed churches, any verifiable authority of the Church's infallibility and Luther himself insisted that if there were no articulations of faith there could be no real confession of faith.[21] It is clear, then, that Protestantism is, like Catholicism, challenged by the difficulties presented by linguistic analysis to the concept of infallibility.

According to the Roman Catholic view, the Church's "remaining in the truth" is above all an interiorization of God's promise of grace in the Church. None the less, the presence of infallibility in all believers as a surprise, in the Protestant sense, is also a fundamental aspect of the Catholic view of infallibility. The whole "body of the faithful, anointed as they are by the Holy One, cannot err in matters of belief". the Second Vatican Coun-

[19] I have even met Catholics who thought that the nomination of a bishop by the Pope was an "infallible" act.
[20] See, for example, E. Jüngel, *Unterwegs zur Sache* (Munich, 1972), p. 195.
[21] *De servo arbitrio*, 1225 (WA 18, 603, 28–9).

cil declared.[22] The Holy Spirit is always present in the whole community's confession and practice of faith, the truth surprising us by being present not only in the official Church. The so-called Protestant view, then, is really a universally Christian *consensus* and it is this fundamental form of the Church's infallibility that provides the key to all other forms, including the dogma as defined by the First Vatican Council (DS 3074).

In universal consensus with all the Christian churches, then, the Roman Catholic Church goes on to speak of the "infallibility of office", the subject of which is, on the one hand, the world episcopate in unity with the Pope and, on the other, the Pope in communion with the world's bishops and the universal faith of all Christians. According to the definition of Vatican I (DS 3074), infallibility is not so much concerned with the material content of the articulation of faith as such as with the meaning of the statement by the Church's teaching office (DS 3020). Certain acts or judgments by certain persons or authoritative bodies are called "infallible" when they are made *ex cathedra* and this term is more precisely defined as concerning the Pope when he speaks as the pastor and teacher formally of *all* believers in defining what is expressed as *revealed*.[23] The First Vatican Council did not *define*, however, if there is a papal—or conciliar—definition *ex cathedra*.[24] In one of the official *Notificationes* appended to the Constitution on the Church of the Second Vatican Council and answering a question about the "theological qualification" to be attached to the constitution, the commission of theologians declared: "As is self-evident, the Council's text must always be interpreted in accordance with the general rules which are known to all".[25]

The statement made in this *Notificatio* confronts us with the very real and difficult problem of the "meta-language", in other

[22] Constitution *Lumen gentium* on the Church, 12.
[23] I agree with G. Thils that the Church's definitions, with or without an *anathema*, about truths that are *not* revealed are not included in the statements which the First Vatican Council *intended* to be regarded as *ex cathedra*; see G. Thils, *L'infaillibilité pontificale* (Gembloux, 1969), pp. 234-46.
[24] See W. Kasper, *op. cit.* (footnote 18), p. 368.
[25] *Constitutiones, Decreta, Declarationes* (Conc. Vat. II) (Vatican City, 1966), p. 214.

words, the statement about a statement. If an "infallible" statement is made, we can only be certain about the infallibility of
that statement if we are told at another time in an infallible way
that it is an infallible statement. Otherwise, we can, according
to the rules of the meta-language, only know in a fallible way
whether the concrete statement is intended by the Church to be
infallible. Expressed in this way, of course, the problem of infallibility would seem to be insoluble. Vatican I was, however,
not aware of this particular problem—it lay outside the historical
context of the Council's questioning and understanding. For the
time being, we may say that later history has shown clearly
enough that, whatever the significance of Vatican I may have
been, it did not or could not answer questions that are now, a
century later, extremely important.

Since Vatican I, Heidegger's "truth does not originally reside
in the *statement*"[26] inevitably reminds the Catholic theologian
of Thomas Aquinas' "the act of faith is ultimately directed towards what is expressed (the *res*), not towards the formula itself
(*enuntiabile*) in which it is expressed".[27] This extremely "modern"
statement of the medieval theologian has often been quoted, but
usually outside the context in which it was originally made.
Thomas wrote with two contemporary ways of thinking in mind
—illuminism, which stressed man's wordless approach to the
mystery, and "rationalism", which emphasized the articulation
of truth. His own position was between these two extremes:
"secundum aliquid *utrumque* est verum";[28] in other words, there
is an element of truth in both ways of thinking, and neither
should be lost. It is above all a question of the mystery itself, but,
Thomas insisted, this mystery has to be approached through the
medium of historical articulation, in which the *res* itself is, im-
perfectly perhaps, expressed. Through our relative historical
articulations (*enuntiabilia*), we reach the truth (*attingere veri-
tatem*), which is never possessed, but only "aimed at" and which
is a *docta ignorantia*, a "negative theology" or conscious un-
knowing which is only possible on the basis of a "positive knowing" that is non-explicit but indirectly expressed in negative dia-

[26] *Vom Wesen der Wahrheit* (Frankfurt, 3rd edn., 1954), p. 12.
[27] *Summa Theologiae*, II–II, q. 1, a. 2, ad 2.
[28] *Op. cit.*, a. 2, in c.

lectics. It is this that bears all knowledge of the truth.[29] In this sense, all judgment of the truth has an irrevocable element, but it has it in a revocable manner.

The Judgment of Truth in a Context of Faith

We can never reach the Absolute *directly* in our consciousness-in-the-world, but we are given it *directly*, as a mystery, in God's revelation of himself, experienced and expressed in the history of the Christian faith, although this gift is made thematically or explicitly only in an *indirect* historical expression. On the basis of this new situation, however, this indirect "secular" expression is qualified inwardly, by virtue of the "light of faith", by the fact that the Absolute is given *directly*. Because of this special event *in* ordinary human structures, the pure conservation of this eschatological content of faith "calls" for the charismatic help of the Spirit.

I would, on this basis, venture to suggest a rather complicated formulation which, I believe, both guarantees the real *meaning* of the dogma of infallibility in a completely *Catholic* way and at the same time also does full justice to the *historicity* of the Christian confession of faith. It is this. In its offices or ministries (the papacy, the episcopate, etc.), the Church is able, at a given moment and within a concrete historical context of understanding, to express the Christian confession of faith *correctly*, *legitimately*, *faithfully* and with authoritative *binding* force. It can do this even though such concepts as "infallible", "irrevocable" and *ex sese* are disputable as historically situated terms implying a certain view of truth and belonging to a certain ecclesiological context. It can also do it although no concrete formulation or articulation (*enuntiabile*) can claim to stand up to the test of time.

If the promise of God's help is to be at all meaningful in history, those holding office must therefore have authority to define Christian faith *here and now*. The articulation of this judgment will, however, always be conditioned by history. We may go further and say that the mystery of Christ will also

---

[29] See my article, "The Value of our Speech about God and of our Concepts of Faith", in *Concept of Truth and Theological Renewal* (London and Sydney, 1968), pp. 5–29.

usually be expressed in a negative, indirect way, at any given moment in history, that is, by the exclusion of a concrete alternative, although this generally takes place through the medium of a concrete affirmation of another alternative.

An example of this is the Tridentine definition of original sin, which says that all men sin "not like Adam" or "not by imitation of Adam", but "by reproduction" (*generatione*) from a sinful human race (DS 790; see also DS 418, 102, 103a). The statement "not by imitation", taken together with the statement "by reproduction", which was, at the time of Trent, all that was considered important, does not *per se* exclude other alternatives which were at that time not envisaged for anthropological reasons. It is clear that "by reproduction" was also intended by the Tridentine dogma on the basis of what was primarily intended, namely, "not by imitation". Since dogmatic statements are expressed in universally human concepts that are not in themselves dogmatic, it is, in a later situation of changed anthropological attitudes, where, for example, the "not by imitation" can be safeguarded by other meaningful models and the "by reproduction" is no longer required, possible for the articulation of a dogma to be discarded without any necessary denial of the dogma itself.

This is a clear indication of the fact that even a so-called infallible definition is an *historical* event in the Church and that it is, precisely as an historical event, subject to the "official charism of the truth" (DS 3071). Not to choose one of the implied alternatives in the historical question about the content of faith at a given moment in history, when faithfulness to the Gospel is at stake, might be tantamount to failing to give an historically faithful answer to the meaningful question: "But who do you say that I am?" (Mark 8. 29; Matt. 16. 15; Luke 9. 20). This is inevitably reminiscent of Paul Ricoeur's comment on the painful necessity to choose, in the vicissitudes of history, the positive in the sadness of the finite. There is no absolute way of answering this question and, because the relationship with the present context of understanding is also *co*-determinative with regard to the faithful answer to the question, no answer in its materially literal sense, that is, outside its context of questioning, is irrevocably the ultimate answer that will be valid for all time. On the other hand, as a faithful answer at a given time and within a given context of understanding, the dogmatic answer is certainly our model, our norm when we attempt to give an answer in a different historical situation.

If, then, God does not help those holding office in the Church to express, within a concrete historical context of understanding, the Christian confession of faith correctly, legitimately, faithfully and with binding force, his promise that the Church will "remain in the truth" will remain empty. It is in connection with this kind of judgment borne by the full charism of the Church's office that the Roman Catholic Church has used the term "infallibility", which is ultimately the infallible guidance of the Holy Spirit manifested in an imperfect historical objectivization in the Church. It would, I think, be much more suitable now, in a different historical context of understanding, to speak of a correct, legitimate judgment concerning faith which is faithful to the Gospel and ultimately binding on all believers. This concept would be more acceptable than the term "infallibility", which is surrounded by ideological and sociological difficulties that seem almost insoluble. The significance of a statement about faith is, after all, partly determined at least by how it functions in practice and a correct dogma may well function wrongly in the life of the Church.

What, then, is its concrete value as truth? (I use the word "concrete" advisedly here and am not referring to its "abstract" truth.) The unity of theory and practice therefore needs to be reformulated if a dogma is to function correctly and this only happens when the dogma is subjected to the criticism of the totality of faith within the whole of history.

Two factors need to be preserved in the reformulation. On the one hand, the lasting confession of faith of the universal Church contains a dogmatic judgment about faith on the part of those holding office. (This aspect was called "infallibility" by the First Vatican Council.) On the other hand, this "infallibility of office" and the "indefectibility" of the community of believers form a structural and organic unity but are distinguished from each other, despite the fact that the "consensus of the Church" itself is expressed in the judgment of those in office. The Pope and the bishops are, in this, subject to the Word of God and to the norm of that Word from which the whole community of believers lives.[30]

Two factors are similarly present in the Catholic hermeneutical circle. On the one hand, dogma is interpreted with Scripture constantly in mind. This means on the one hand that Scripture always forms part of the context within which any given dogma is understood. On the other hand, Scripture is at the same time always brought into relationship with dogma. Every dogmatic definition has therefore to be interpreted not only by using the method of historical and literary criticism of the text and its historical and social context, but also within the unity of the total history of faith beginning with Scripture. If it is not clearly appreciated that dogmatic definitions are conditioned by this non-dogmatic context of understanding which is neither revealed nor "infallible", the purely material repetition of an early dogma can result in a complete misunderstanding of the teaching that the Church at that time wished to safeguard.

Translated by David Smith

[30] Dogmatic Constitution *Dei Verbum* on Revelation, 10.

IV. Peter as the Foundation Stone in the Present Uncertainty

René Laurentin

TO CLARIFY the role of the successor of Peter in the order of truth and certainty constitutes a very pressing "pastoral"[1] problem, at a time when Christians feel very insecure and are therefore all too ready for contestation, defection or the hardening of intransigent attitudes. It is, therefore, essential to define the meaning and scope of this guarantee given by Christ to the apostles and more especially to Peter. Before doing this, however, a number of ambiguities must be cleared up.

I. THE DIALECTICS OF INFALLIBILITY

Whenever this question arises, one highly charged word inevitably presents itself—infallibility. Chosen by Pius IX, in the spirit of contestation with which he confronted his own century, for the definition of 1870, this word made an extraordinary impact and it is still a focus of interest both within the Roman Church and outside it. It is significant that the book in which Hans

---

[1] This is not the place to discuss the ambiguities of the word "pastoral", which indicates the point of view from which this article is written. At the Council, it became a kind of Trojan horse, leaders of both the majority and the minority groups claiming that pastoral theology was distinct from doctrine as such. The former thus contrived to introduce, under cover of this innocent word, a complete theological renewal, unfortunately very badly co-ordinated with a doctrinal system which, in appearance, remained intact. Today we are still far from having disposed of this ambiguity, which is built into the texts of Vatican II. All genuine theology is pastoral theology and what is genuinely pastoral is also theological.

Küng invites us to substitute the notion of *indefectibility* for that of *infallibility* takes the second, none the less, as its title.[2] "Indefectible" produces scarcely any effect, but "infallible" still has the power to shock, even a century after the definition of Vatican I and in spite of the extreme moderation with which the Holy See celebrated the centenary.[3] In the repertoire of theological literature, "infallibility" is rather like those old plays which manage to succeed as box-office draws each time they are revived. The fact is that this word touches on themes and myths vitally present to the heart of man: truth, error, today, "becomingness", all of routine concern for the specialists, although the "becomingness" of creation still poses certain problems.

God is infallible. Can man be so too, either by participation or delegation? Can he challenge history, which has, in effect, destroyed or proved to be relative so many former certainties, reduced now to the condition of ethnological or cultural curiosities?

Infallibility—this peremptory word commends itself by virtue of the very power inherent in the dogma, for the function of dogma is not merely to define and clarify, but to evoke a response, to express, in words of human wisdom, that power to affirm which belongs to the testimony of God and the impact of his foolishness which is wiser than men (1 Cor. 1. 25). This term has above all set afoot a debate which is bearing considerable fruit in the shape of lively discussions and unexpected changes of position. The irony is that their very insistence on this word has turned against the ambitious designs of those who urged it so forcefully. The infallible definition of infallibility reduced both the content of the idea and the possibility of exercising the charism.

On the one hand, such a great power is formidable. Soon after the definition of 1870, Wilfrid Monod said: "It is such a weighty canon, that no one will dare make use of it." In fact, one papal definition has been promulgated since then—the Assumption in

[2] Hans Küng, *Infallible? An Enquiry* (London, 1971).
[3] To mark the centenary there was no solemnity. The Holy See more or less restricted itself to publishing, without preface or commemorative text, a selection of articles published between 1946 and 1964 by men respected for their courage in the scientific and ecumenical fields, Dom Lambert Bauduin, A. Chavasse, B. Dejaifve, J. Hamer, G. Thils, in a book entitled *De doctrina de Concili primi* (Rome, 1969).

1950, which Pius XII only defined after he had given up the idea of defining the universal mediation of Mary, a project thwarted by the objections of the Holy Office. Regarding the Assumption, he affirmed only the minimum, namely that Mary had been *taken up* (*assumpta*), body and soul, with the risen Christ. Nothing more, either about death or immortality, when or how, "going up" into "heaven", or even any "unique privilege" enjoyed by Mary, such as that claimed for the Immaculate Conception by Pius IX in 1854, was defined. Since then, Vatican II deliberately avoided making any definition, and Paul VI struck out, with his own hand, the phrase *infallibili auctoritate*, which the drafters of *Humanae Vitae* had proposed to him. Infallibility, like the tiara, lies heavy on the head of him who wears it.

The conciliar discussions which preceded the definition of infallibility reduced the scope of this ambitious word. To promulgate it within limits consistent with revelation and to get it past the vote in an assembly whose governing principle was moral unanimity, it was necessary to restrict its meaning in a way that calls to mind the English proverb: one sometimes has to shave one's head in order not to lose one's hair. Since infallibility cannot admit any kind of contradiction without the risk of self-destruction, it could only be defined in an emasculated form, on a strictly juridical basis.

During Vatican I, the more warlike spirits among the leaders of the majority clung tenaciously to three epithets. For them, it was a matter of defining an *absolute, isolated* and *personal* infallibility and the point was even reached when some of the Council Fathers were saying that just as there was the council of the three chapters, so Vatican I will be the council of the three adjectives.[4] The final definition positively excluded the two former epithets and lessened the ambiguity of the third.

1. Infallibility is not absolute

In many ways, papal infallibility is brought into perspective by the definition of Vatican I and by the authorized explanations of the official secretary, Mgr V. Gasser, who clarified the terms submitted to the vote. Infallibility is neither "political" nor "scientific", but merely doctrinal. According to the very terms

[4] Mgr B. d'Avanzo, Mansi, 52, 761a.

of the definition, it is limited to occasions, that is, when the Pope speaks *ex cathedra*, when, that is, "in virtue of his supreme apostolic authority", he exercises "the office of shepherd and teacher of all Christians", not when he speaks as a private individual, or as bishop of the diocese of Rome; also when he "defines", formally, "doctrine to be held by the universal Church" (Constitution *Pastor aeternus*, c. 4, "definition", Denzinger 3074), and that only when this doctrine concerns "faith or morals", to the exclusion, therefore, of secular matters and private opinions.

The further explanations given by the Council impose the following restrictions. Infallibility is not omniscience or a miraculous second sight. It does not rely, as does Scripture, on inspiration, but depends on help from God which preserves certain solemn acts from error. Infallible definitions are the word of the pope, and not the word of God. This help is "entirely negative in character".[5] It prevents the pope from "teaching in a definitively binding way anything contrary to divine truth".[6] Papal infallibility is not magic. "The pope is obliged to use every appropriate means for searching out the truth and suitably expressing it", declared Mgr Gasser, the official secretary of the Council. Papal infallibility is not arbitrary, but totally subject to revelation, of which the pope is simply the interpreter. He must conform to it, and can neither propose nor countenance any new public revelation. Progress in the human sciences over the past century has, moreover, manifested the relative nature of language and culture.

2. *Infallibility is not isolated*

Although the help of God is neither mediated nor juridically controlled by human authorities, papal infallibility cannot be taken in isolation from the rest of the Church or located outside it. "We do not separate the Roman Pontiff from the Church to which he is closely bound", declared Mgr Gasser (Mansi 52, 1213b). According to the definition, the pope is infallible only in the exercise of his "office as shepherd and teacher" in and for the Church. The infallibility of the pope is neither isolated nor

[5] L. Bouyer, *L'Eglise de Dieu* (Paris, 1970), p. 443.
[6] K. Rahner and H. Vorgrimler, *Concise Theological Dictionary* (London, 1965), p. 228.

exclusive. Mgr Gasser rejected the amendment of the Bishop of Urgel, according to which no infallibility would be recognized in the Church apart from that which is communicated to it by the pope (Mansi 52, 1222c). The definition, furthermore, makes it very clear that the infallibility of the Roman Pontiff is the exercise by the pope of that *infallibility with which the divine Redeemer willed that his Church should be endowed for the defining of doctrine concerning faith or morals* (Denzinger 3064).

What Vatican I defined was the ability of the pope to make use, without juridical control, of that primary infallibility, which all attribute without discussion to the episcopate and to the Church as a whole. He is its chief organ, and the organ cannot be separated from the organism.

3. *Infallibility is functional*

Is this infallibility personal? This equivocal expression was criticized at the First Vatican Council.[7] It is by virtue not of his person, but of his office, that the pope enjoys the infallible help of God. As a private individual he can make mistakes like anyone else.

If the third epithet cannot be rejected outright, like the other two, this is because the word "infallible" qualifies not so much a *proposition* as the *judgment* made about it and, in this sense, the mind that makes the judgment. The exercise of the function of infallibility depends on a person and is proper to that person in so far as he exercises the function. If the pope may not be separated from the Church, no more can the infallible role he exercises be separated from him. This would be merely another way of side-stepping the issue.

At all events, this last adjective aroused sufficient feelings of reserve to prevent the Council from using it. An intervention by Cardinal Guidi, moreover, served to effect a change in the original title of the Dogmatic Constitution (chapter 4) from *De romani pontificis infallibilitate* (Mansi 52, 6) to *De romani ponti-*

---

[7] Cf. B. d'Avanzo, Mansi, 52, 762d. J. P. Torrell, "L'infaillibilité pontificale est-elle un privilège personnel?", in *Revue des Sciences Philosophiques et Théologiques*, 45 (1961), pp. 229–45, reproduced in *De doctrina Concilii Vaticani Primi* (Rome, 1969), pp. 488–505.

ficis infallibili magisterio (Denzinger 3065; and the explanation by Gasser in Mansi 52, 1218D, 1219A).

The ideology of the "infallibilists" was thus robbed of its force in the very definition of infallibility. Nothing of it remains, except the *ex sese*, whose strictly juridical bearing was brought within its narrow limits by Vatican II (see G. Dejaifve, "Ex sese", in *Salesianum* 24, 1962, pp. 283–95). In order to find our way out of this maze, we must begin by clarifying the origins and bearing of this ideology.

II. REVELATION AND IDEOLOGY: THE HISTORICAL PERSPECTIVE

The state of the problem is this: revelation and ideology cannot be oversimplified, as if it were just a question of stripping away the ideology to rediscover the revelation. On the one hand, the ideology performs the necessary historical function of giving concrete form to the mission envisaged by Christ. We cannot simply reject "ideology" and "myth". Rather, it should be our concern to establish both the limitations and the scope of these humble instruments of all human understanding. On the other hand, it would be quite unrealistic to compare the harshness of the ideologies with the persuasive gentleness of revelation. Christ's words, promising protection to his Church and to Peter, are abrupt and challenging: "He who hears you hears me" (Lk. 10. 16, etc.). "You are Peter, and on this rock I will build my church" (Mt. 16. 18, etc.). What concerns us here is the kind of ideology that inspires those dialectical and impassioned conflicts, which we must always try to resolve.

1. *The Middle Ages*

It first emerged, during the reign of Gregory VII, as the ideology of a special manifestation of power. At a time when interference by the secular authorities was corrupting the whole Church by subjugating it to the powers of this world, the papacy became aware of its responsibility. Alone, therefore, and in the name of God, it rose up to confront those powers. Steeled and fortified, it armed itself with weapons suited to the conflict, setting itself above the emperor himself. All this is expressed in the *dictatus papae*, the twenty-seven brief, lapidary principles formulated by Gregory VII in 1075:

1. The Roman Church was founded by the Lord alone.
2. Only the Roman Pontiff can rightly be called universal.
3. He alone can depose and absolve bishops.
4. At a Council, his legate ranks above all the bishops, even when he is of inferior rank, and only he can pronounce a sentence of deposition against them.
7. Only the pope can establish new laws.
8. He alone has control over the insignia of the empire.
9. The pope is the only man whose feet are kissed by princes.
11. His name is unique throughout the world.
12. He is empowered to depose emperors.
18. No one may alter his sentence; he alone may alter those of others.
19. No one can pass judgment on him.
22. The Roman Church has never erred, and, as Scripture bears witness, will never be able to err.
23. The Roman Pontiff, once he is canonically ordained, becomes *ipso facto* holy, through the merits of St Peter. . . .

This ideological and political position was relevant in a civilization for which all power was sacred, all power hierarchical; where there was scarcely any other alternative for the successor of St Peter but to be enslaved or to dominate, however unfitting might be the establishment of the ministry of Peter as a secular power.

What interests us here, however, is not the heritage of the Roman Empire, which the pope (*summus pontifex*) thus took up, but rather the hierarchical and theocratic origins of the ideology which developed.

To describe the process, T. Strotmann[8] has spoken of "cephalization", a formula inspired by Innocent III, which plays on the relation between the Hebrew *keph* (*kephas*), rock, and the Greek *kephalē*, head: "Although in the one language *kephas* is translated as 'rock', in the other it means 'head' . . . the head possesses the fullness of the senses, whilst the other members receive only a part of this fullness. . . ."[9]

[8] T. Strotmann, "Primauté et céphalisation", in *Irenikon*, 37 (1964), pp. 187–97.
[9] Cf. *De sacro altaris mysterio* I, 8, PL 217, 778; Y. Congar, "Cephas-Cephale-Caput", in *Revue du Moyen-Age latin*, 8 (1952), pp. 5–42.

This metaphor of the head, which Scripture applies only to Christ, and never to the other ministers, is taken as a point of departure for attributing to Peter and his successors all the properties of the head in a body. Thus the Sovereign Pontiff has been made the principle of the Church: "in the organic sense of the later treatise *De Christo Capite*. For the popes Rome is *caput*, a *source*, that is, from which everything else flows. *Caput* takes on the value of *fons*."[10]

All prerogatives, then, came to be concentrated in the pope as the apex of the hierarchical pyramid. He was invested on the one hand with the powers and prerogatives both of the episcopate and of the people, and on the other with the power and infallibility of God. The pope came to be identified with Christ. He was thought of less and less as the successor of Peter and more and more as the successor and vicar of Jesus Christ, whom Hervé Nedellec (d. 1323) considered to be the first pope (Y. Congar, *Ministères*, Paris 1971, p. 13). He became, in the words of St Catherine of Siena, "the sweet Christ on earth". He was identified, verbally at least, with God himself.[11] Victor Hugo conveys some idea of this sacralizing and divinizing process when he speaks of "those two halves of God, the pope and the emperor". But according to the medieval texts, the pope is "the God of the emperor" (*Deus imperatoris, ibid.*, pp. 278 and 287). This concentration of the plenitude of God and of the Church, as power and authority, in the visible person of Peter was analogous with that realized in the person of Mary on the mystical plane.[12]

[10] Other references in Y. Congar, *L'Ecclésiologie du haut Moyen-Age* (Paris, 1968), pp. 192–3; G. Thils, *La primauté pontificale* (Gembloux, 1972), pp. 180–90.

[11] J. Rivière, "Sur l'expression Papa-Deus au Moyen-Age", in *Miscellanea*; F. Ehrle, Vol. 2, *Per la storia di Roma* (Rome, 1424), pp. 276–89. The author quotes the Protestant monographs which have collated the material relevant to this process of divinization, and sets out to limit the scope of the texts cited. The etymological development is indicative of the ideology and of the mythical substratum. Compare this with the analogous development whose object was the Virgin Mary, and see the following note.

[12] For the attribution of the title of goddess to the Virgin Mary, one will find references on the Catholic side in H. Marraci, *Polyanthea Mariana* (Rome, 1685), republished by J. Bourasse in *Summa aurea*, 9 (1862), col. 1085; on the Protestant side in C. Drelincourt, *Demandes sur la qualité de l'honneur qui est dû à la sainte et bienheureuse Vierge Marie,*

2. After Vatican I

At the Second Vatican Council, on 5 December 1962, in order to teach a salutary lesson, Maximos IV quoted the following text: "The pope is God on earth . . . Jesus has set the pope above the prophets, above his precursor . . . above the angels. . . . Jesus has placed the pope on a level with God" (*L'Eglise melkite au Concile*, Beirut, 1967, pp. 75–6). Maximos IV had been careful not to give his reference explicitly, so that even the Curia was puzzled about the possible depths from which the patriarch could have drawn up such a text. Its authorship was traced, in fact, to a canonized saint: John Bosco (*Meditazioni*, Vol. 1, 2nd edn., pp. 89–90). And the text had presented no difficulty during the process of canonization.

But such excesses relate to a further stage, that in which the ideology of power, developed by the fourteenth-century canonists, became popular. How did the development take place? The one-sided investing of all prerogatives and powers in the person of the pope, frustrated for a time by the Great Schism and then by the lapses of certain Renaissance popes, was resumed unhindered once the papacy had coped with its internal crisis, could give once more an example of moral rectitude and had shaken itself free of the temporal burden which compromised its spiritual influence. Henceforth, the main bulwark against excesses and false ideologies would be the definition of Vatican I.

Although it was ultimately doomed, one possibility of survival was left to this ideology. Spurred on by their apparent triumph, the champions of infallibility had recourse to a procedure then in vogue: they started from the concept of infallibility taken *in itself*, in order to draw from it all the consequences possible, just as the medievals had done with the image of the head, which they took for granted as traditional. "Infallibilization" underwent the same treatment as "cephalization". In this way, the

---

2nd edn. (Charenton, 1644. Bibliothèque Nationale D2 3804), pp. 45–68. The Virgin was also subjected to a certain process of "cephalization", even to the point when she was called "secondary head of the mystical body" or *concaput*. But if almost every title of Christ was accorded to the Virgin, in fact it was, above all, the operations of the Holy Spirit that were attributed to her: immediate source of all grace, and principle of the growth of Christ in souls. See R. Laurentin, "Marie et l'Esprit Saint", in *Nouvelle revue théologique*, 89 (1967), pp. 26–42, especially pp. 26–31.

idea that the pope is infallible in all the acts of his ordinary magisterium was developed.[13] Although it has always been treated with reserve by experts, this idea was fairly widespread in official circles, and among the ordinary Christians, who imagine, even today, that "encyclicals are infallible". This misapprehension is shared by other Christians who have not as yet been enlightened by the ecumenical dialogue. These developments in the spirit of Vatican I took shape by means of a logical and a mythical process.

On the logical plane, the schema of "alone" and "all" was worked out. The pope *alone* has *all* power in the Church. He came to be seen as the *only* principle of *all* jurisdiction and no power existed, except his. These novelties tended to gain acceptance because what the pope had done *sometimes* he could *always* do, and it is fitting that he should, since the Church would be purer if everything in it flowed from that one pure source, "the Holiness of our Lord", as the pope was then called. This process, and others, have been studied in detail by G. Thils in his book, *La primauté pontificale* (Gembloux, 1972), pp. 188–98. Following the same line of thought, some theologians maintained that the infallibility of the Council was *conferred* by the pope *alone*, as a participation in the fullness of his personal power.

The myths and rituals of this ideology proliferated under Pius XII. The object of the Roman pilgrimage became less and less to visit the tomb of the apostles, more and more "to see the pope". The papal entourage encouraged pilgrims to intensify their acclamations of the Sovereign Pontiff. When he passed by on the *sedia gestatoria*, all competed to touch him, or to get him to touch some object. He would even co-operate in the ritual exchange of skull caps, which were soon being mass-produced in unofficial workshops. The pilgrims would hold one out to Pius XII when he passed on the *sedia*, and he would give them, in exchange, the one he had on his head, a precious relic of the Sovereign Pontiff. The *Osservatore Romano* never mentioned his name without prefacing it with the adjective *illuminato*, or something similar.

---

[13] The infallibility of the ordinary magisterium has been upheld by Vacant, *Le Magistère ordinaire de l'Eglise et ses organes* (Paris, 1889), especially pp. 97–116. Other references will be found in Y. Congar, *Ministères et communion ecclésiale* (Paris, 1971), p. 151.

John XXIII put a stop to all such rituals at the beginning of his pontificate.

This emphasis on a simple, personal symbol caught on more readily among the masses than did the subtle distinctions of the theologians. It gave them the reassuring sense of having discovered, in a tangible and familiar form, the living image of the unseen Christ. It fostered an attitude of obedience founded on reverence and love for God, mediated through the head of the Church. But this totalitarian concept of the magisterium and of the primacy had its drawbacks.

To make the papal magisterium the universal rule of faith, as was done in an article by one of the official theologians of the time, *Il magisterio vivo di SS Pio XII, norma prossima e universale di verità*,[14] was to reduce Scripture to the state of a remote and insufficient norm, as Père de Broglie courageously observed at the time (Preface to L. Bouyer, *Du Protestantisme à l'Eglise*, Paris, 1951). It also meant that theologians, according to the directives of *Humani generis*, were restricted to repeating the encyclicals.

From another point of view, this totalitarianism served to encourage, in those who wielded the power, a megalomania quite out of keeping with evangelical humility, and brought the people to that state of irresponsible passivity summed up in Brunetière's maxim: "Go and inquire of Rome what I believe." According to such a maxim, faith was present in the Holy See, but for Christians in general it had a merely extrinsic value, expressed as blind and unconditional obedience to what was believed by Peter. All that was known, professed and experienced by the believer was of no importance. People relied on this sense of security, to the detriment of the vitality of faith.

3. *Vatican II*

The important thing here is the positive source of contemporary reappraisal—Vatican II. Many of the Fathers present openly challenged the "pyramidal" view of the Church, according to which "the pope is all, the people nothing", and Vatican II restored the priority of communion over hierarchy. Whereas

[14] L. Ciappi in *Sapienza*, 7 (1954), pp. 125-51.

the leaders of Vatican I insisted on absolute dependence on the pope,[15] Vatican II recalled that the people do not exist for the pope but that the pope exists for the people, whose servant he is. This Copernican revolution restored the significance, both of Christ's role in the Spirit, and the responsibility of Christians in the Church. At a single blow, it destroyed all absolutist, juridical or rigid notions of the pontifical magisterium.

Is this a revolution in the etymological sense of an upheaval which rejects the past? No: truth does not emerge from elimination and contradiction. The old formulae (and in the first place, those of the definitions of 1870, including the *ex sese*, as elucidated by Vatican II) preserve their value on the *juridical* plane to which they belong. At this level, the people of God are dependent on the authority of the pope as aided by Christ. But in the context of their *organic* relationship, the pope is at the service of the people—he is complemented by them, as an organ by the entire body, in order to express their authentic faith. Vatican II completes what Vatican I said about the juridical dependence, by pointing out the interdependence and organic solidarity essential for the vitality of the Church.

Let us now try, in this perspective, to describe the office of Peter's successor, such as it can be rightfully taught, understood and lived among the people of God.

III. THE FUNCTION OF THE SUCCESSOR OF PETER AS SERVANT OF THE UNITY OF FAITH

1. *A Function in and for the Church*

In the first place, the function of Peter and his successors is situated within the Church, not outside and above it. It is an organic function in a living body. It is principally to the Church, in fact, that Christ promised indefectibility (Mt. 28. 30; Jn. 14. 26; 16. 13), and it is in the context of the Church, against whom "the gates of hell shall not prevail", that the promises made to Peter (Mt. 16. 18; cf. Lk. 22, 32; Jn. 21. 15–17) or to the apostles

---

[15] Mgr B. d'Avanzo, Archbishop of Calvi, strongly insisted on this "absolute dependence". He repeated the expression several times, both in connection with the total subordination of the apostles to Peter, and with that of the bishops to the pope. Mansi, 53, pp. 713–15; G. Thils, *La primauté pontificale* (Gembloux, 1972), pp. 164–5.

as a body, find their place (Constitution, *Lumen Gentium*, on the Church). The passing on of the faith is not the exclusive function of the pope. It is a task for the Church as a whole, as Vatican II has reminded us (Constitution, *Dei Verbum*, on Revelation).

The function of the Twelve (and of the ministers who succeed them) is a visible service which aims to safeguard the purity of the channels of salvation; a function of discernment, approved, in the name of Christ himself, for the purpose of sustaining and interpreting the faith and the evangelical spirit in the face of the changes brought by time and the ravages of sin. The function of Peter's successor within the episcopate is the visible service of unity, through the exercise of an authority which counteracts error, and in the last resort guarantees the judgment and true discernment mentioned above. It is because of this that he receives help from God to act at the universal level.

His task is therefore to judge before God what means should be employed for the discharge of his office. During the first centuries, his function was to reconcile by arbitrating in conflicts, by enacting measures for the public safety in times of emergency, and also by providing an example. What is more, the churches recognized as exemplary, not the person of the bishop of Rome, but the faith of that Church, founded on the confession of Peter and Paul.

If this reconciling function has today adopted an administrative form, which swamps the Church with offices, directives and regulations and maintains control over everything, this is only a recent and special form of this function. It can avoid the making of mistakes, and guarantees a certain type of homogeneity. It has the defect of relying on structures, whereas Christ entrusted everything to the Spirit and to man, although he knew well "what was in man" (Jn. 2. 25). Such a system is better equipped to guarantee the authenticity of a *deposit* than that of a *movement*; the stability of structures, rather than fidelity to the Gospel; the preservation of material acquisitions, rather than the urgency of the inner demand and the missionary thrust.

2. *A Service in and for Faith*

The role of Peter only makes sense in this context. It is at the service of faith and love and is rooted in a confession of faith at

Caesarea (Mt. 16. 16) and of love at Genesareth (Jn. 21. 15). Thus, even though Peter's role is partly juridical, this must be understood in its relation to its essential function. It is not, indeed, a question of a blank cheque given to a signing-clerk, according to the juridical practice of this world. Christ vigorously contrasted the "service" of the apostles with the lordship and authority (*exousia*) of kings.

The pope does not inherit a ready-made authority, but rather an organic mission to be exercised in faith and love in his humble condition as sinner. This is why Christ severely reprimanded Peter, just established in his position as foundation stone (Mt. 16. 18), saying to him: "Get behind me, Satan! You are a hindrance to me; for you are not on the side of God but of men" (Mt. 16. 23). Christ does not sanction all the human thoughts of Peter and his successors. The task of confirming his brethren was also given to Peter with a definite reference to his previous fall: "When you have turned again (*epistrepsas*), strengthen your brethren"; and the invitation to a triple confession of love: "Do you love me more than these?" (Jn. 21. 15–17), is offered as a means of reconciliation for the triple denial.

3. *A Service subordinate to Revelation*

The function of Peter is intrinsically bound up with the revelation of Christ. The pope, like every Christian, is completely subject to it. Even in the exercise of his office, he is its servant, not its master. He can add nothing to this revelation. He would no longer be acting within the limits of his role if, *per impossibile*, he conceived the idea of making a new revelation. This would simply be subject to Paul's admonition to the Galatians in 1. 8: "If an angel from heaven should preach to you a gospel contrary to that which we preached to you, let him be accursed." It is this lower limit which is expressed concretely by the classic hypothesis of the heretical pope; at the opposite pole is the upper limit, embodied in the infallible definitions.

Subject to the objective data of revelation, which are transmitted through Scripture and the very life of the indefectible Church, the pope is personally responsible to the light that comes to him from the Spirit. He is infallible only as the witness of an infallible God, and in so far as he has been *sent* as his witness.

4. *A Service going beyond Infallible Formulae*

Here a fundamental question must be added—in what sense is the function of Peter concerned with truth as such? The decadent theology of the past few centuries, admittedly inspired by a praiseworthy concern for precision and clarity, tended to distinguish, on the one hand, the truth of dogmas considered purely as formulae and, on the other, practical attitudes considered as simple consequences or applications of this truth. People thus came to accept these juridical norms as principles of life and action, when in fact they are but guidelines.

The unilateral progression which leads from truth to action is the inverse of that to be found in John 3. 20: "He who does what is true comes to the light." Today, this second progression has been restored to favour. In fact, the revelation of Jesus is not presented as a body of doctrine, but as the manifestation and outpouring of *agapē*: the love of God and the love which he communicates to men. He reveals this, moreover, in his own person and in his actions more completely than in his words. Certainly love implies some knowledge, which can be formulated in doctrinal terms, but this doctrine of salvation was worked out later, and would be quite meaningless apart from the *agapē* which defines the very nature both of God and of salvation.

There is no question of placing life and truth in opposition to one another. They are correlatives, and neither can be treated as a mere by-product of the other. Orthopraxis is more important than orthodoxy, according to the parable of the two sons. What is more, no orthodoxy can survive apart from orthopraxis, for erroneous practice contradicts the word and brands it as untruth. The mission of Peter's successor, then, is not confined to the authentification of speculative truths. It reaches out to the indivisible combination of love and knowledge. Integrity of life and action is not less important than certain knowledge, nor is it separable from it.

This function, which the pope exercises on a world-wide scale, and whose specific task is the preservation of unity, is not restricted to the promulgation of infallible definitions, but consists also in guiding, directing, correcting, confirming and giving support to faith. It is a matter of safeguarding, through these means, and against all comers, the authenticity of the transmission, which consists of movement. It is essential therefore to assure unity in movement, and, in whatever pluralism there may be, to secure not polarization but convergence, not contradiction but harmony, not disintegration but complementarity.

The anxious concern for security, which gave a privileged place to abstract formulae, and concentrated more specifically on infallible decisions, was therefore disastrous. These are no more than very rare and particular instances of the charism of Peter.

Papal infallibility has been exercised only twice, on both occasions to define privileges of the Virgin Mary, the Immaculate Conception in 1854 and the Assumption in 1950. Both are subsidiary doctrines, and these pronouncements, whose significance was considerably exaggerated in the writing of the time, which implied that they would be vital sources for a new era in the Church, appear in retrospect as of minor importance. Nothing indicates that they have prompted any renewal, even where devotion to Mary is concerned. On the contrary, the definition of the Assumption was followed by a kind of distaste, both for the dogma and for the feast. "Now it is of no further interest to anyone", said one publisher, shortly after the promulgation of the dogma. And in fact, articles on this subject, which until then had been growing in number, suddenly seemed to dry up. The importance of infallible definitions in the life of the Church is therefore very restricted. It would be a mistake to exaggerate it. They must not become the tree that prevents us from seeing the forest.

5. *A Service which defines but does not create Certainty in Faith*

Finally, the role of Peter must be interpreted in its relation to the certainty of faith. This point is doubly important for our subject, firstly because Peter was established by Christ as a foundation stone (Mt. 16. 18) and a guarantee of stability as well as of guidance and of pastoral leadership (Jn. 21. 15–18) and secondly because Christians are passing through a crisis of faith at the moment. Once again, the role of Peter must be situated on the low level from which it derives its true value.

Above all, it is necessary to keep in mind the classical doctrine that the assurance of faith rests primarily and directly on the testimony of God in each believer.[16] This testimony does not have the character of an objective revelation. It consists of a light which illuminates, from within, the certainty transmitted objectively by means of words and signs. If this testimony establishes a basic certainty, the obscurity inherent in faith and in the sinful condition of man gives rise to many a failure to discriminate between things as they really are, seen in the light of God, and every sort of mirage. It is to provide a remedy for such human instability that the visible function of the apostles and of Peter was established. But it is not the function of infallibility to *create* certainty in faith, which comes directly from God himself. Its more specific task is to protect, interpret, evaluate, define and authenticate that certainty and to exclude the errors that become intermingled with it.

The light of faith is not an entirely individual phenomenon. It is not just direct contact of God with a series of isolated monads. It is a light given in love, and for the sake of love; a communal light given organically in the community of believers, the body of Christ. The magisterium is a special organ in that body. What characterizes this particular form of service is not so much information and scientific competence, which is proper to the theologians, nor intensity of inner illumination, which is the mark of the saints. The magisterium, which may indeed have its own share of those qualities, has, as its specific task, that of judging and verifying. In the exercise of its function, it draws on that same infallible light of God.

In all this it is essential to locate the absolute and the relative correctly, all the more so today, when, after the centuries during which infallibility was treated as an absolute, we have succumbed to radical and widespread relativizations which leave the believer disorientated and deprived of any reliable point of reference. To recover the meaning of the absolute, we must humbly locate it where in fact it is. For there are false absolutes, such as the death of God, false transcendences, such as cheap materialism or some phallic idol.

[16] 1 Jn. 5. 19; cf. Mt. 11. 25 (inner revelation of God to the poor and the humble); 1 Cor. 2. 9–12 (cf. 2 Cor. 4. 6); Heb. 8. 10–12 (cf. Jer. 31. 33–4); Jn. 6. 45; 14. 26; 16. 12–13; 1 Jn. 2. 20 and 27; 5. 10; see also G. de Broglie, *De Fide*, a course printed by the Institut catholique de Paris (1958), caput 2, pp. 17–40: "De testimonio divino quo fides inititur".

We are no longer suffering today from the illusion that *absolute truth* can be identified with a formula, even an infallible one. St Thomas had no such illusion. He knew well that no formula is more than a sign, and hence a relative means, a pointer for the intentionality of our knowledge of the God who saves. That is what is meant by his dictum, still a source of illumination for us today: "The act of the believer does not end with the article of faith but with the reality".[17] The absolute reality, which is the goal, is the mystery of Christ, or in other words of the God who saves: a mystery "which surpasses knowledge" (Eph. 3. 20; Phil. 4. 7, etc.). This reality is also the *goal of history*, since revelation has hope as its object. Thus Christ is the *way* before being the *truth* (Jn. 14. 6).

The relative nature of these statements of faith in other words has two aspects. In the first place, these statements are relative with regard to the mystery of God which cannot be fully expressed in any formula. However imperfect these formulae may be, on the other hand, we can use them to reach what is essential. Using an inadequate formula, the firm believer may become totally immersed in that reality, while excellent formulae remain obscure to believers who have not really experienced faith. In the same way, the non-expert understands nothing of an excellent radiographic term, while an experienced doctor can come to valuable conclusions on the basis of an inadequate term. By recognizing the limitations of dogmatic formulae, Thomas Aquinas made it possible to evaluate them correctly as a means of attaining to the absolute.

Secondly, the formulae of faith are relative with respect to the future. Revealed truth is, in fact, the truth of *salvation* and hence of an unfulfilled promise. This must be brought to completion through the vital transformation and active co-operation of every believer. In this sense, absolute truth is eschatological. "It is at the end", classical theology was saying, well before Moltmann.

Those who have exaggerated the function of Peter have compromised it in the eyes of Christians, both Catholic and Pro-

[17] *Summa Theologica* II–II, q. 1, a. 2, ad. 2; see also articles 1, 3 (Fidei non potest subesse aliquod falsum), 6 (Sed. contra). Cf. *Sentences*, III, d. 25, q. 1, a. 1, quaestiuncula 1, objection 4. Cf. Y. Congar, *Ministères et communion ecclésiale*, p. 153; E. Schillebeeckx, *Approches théologiques. 1. Révélation et théologie* (Brussels, 1965), pp. 69–76.

testant. It is significant that the extreme Protestant polemicists have deliberately seized on the extreme Catholic arguments about infallibility and have found an ideal Aunt Sally. By way of contrast, the humble way in which John XXIII managed, at the Council, to make a number of interventions designed to foster dialogue between conflicting theological tendencies (on revelation, for example, in December 1962) showed the non-Catholic observers present the real purpose of the office of Peter's successor. One must, therefore, be conscious of the humble status of this office which, along with the others, expresses one way in which the infallible God is present to the Church and to individual believers. This office, which has no meaning outside the context of faith and love, must be acknowledged in a spirit of faith, love and therefore also of humility.

Translated by Sarah Fawcett

PART II
DOCUMENTATION

Anton Houtepen

A Hundred Years after Vatican I: Some Light on the Concept of Infallibility

A HUNDRED years after Vatican I, the debate about the meaning and function of the concept of infallibility has been re-opened, mainly as a result of developments since the Council in ecclesiology and hermeneutics. The present discussion goes far beyond the question as to whether or not the Petrine office is infallible. It is concerned with whether the concept can be applied both to a whole complex of hermeneutical questions and to the entire range of "authorities" in the "system of faith" with which it has traditionally been associated. Many problems which were hardly considered at all during the First Vatican Council therefore have a bearing on the present debate.

In this article, I shall concentrate on recent studies which deal specifically with the concept of infallibility, with the inevitable result that more general hermeneutical and ecclesiological works will be neglected. I shall first consider a number of historical studies connected with the origins of the concept of infallibility. In the second section of this article, I shall discuss works dealing with the dogma itself. I shall then review works which question whether the concept is still useful, and finally I shall consider the debate about Hans Küng's *Infallible? An Enquiry*.

I. THE ORIGINS OF THE CONCEPT OF INFALLIBILITY

Until recently, most writers have dealt with the ecclesiological aspects of this question and very few have considered the historical development of the concept itself.[1] Now, however, it is how and when this concept has been used in the search for norms concerning certainty in what is said by leaders and members of the community of believers that arouses more interest. The book containing the ecumenical discussions held at Chèvetogne in 1961[2] provides several examples of this new interest. Reynders[3] and Dupuy[4] especially show how, from the earliest times, Christians have looked for criteria for their confession of faith and how more and more emphasis has come to be placed on the part played by Church leaders in this search. Similar conclusions can be found in the collection of essays about problems of authority in the Church.[5] Yves Congar has provided a detailed documentation of this development in a book on medieval ecclesiology[6] and another on the Church from Augustine to the present.[7] K. F. Morrison's work is also very instructive.[8]

In the historical development from *auctoritas* to *potestas* (Congar and Tavard) and from *traditio* to *discretio* (Morrison), a process of alienation from the original event has, according to these authors, taken place. Any attempt to make the official testimony authentic by referring to *traditio* (the canon of Scripture and conciliar pronouncements) has to be amplified by a formal legitimation (delegation, *consensus* and *receptio* or else the power of the keys and *successio*). How, then, did the concept of *infallibilis,* which was originally applied firstly to God and secondly to the content of faith in Scripture and the articles of faith, come finally to be applied to the Church's office? De Vooght[9] showed in 1961 that there was no hint of this development before about 1300. It is generally assumed that it began with the question of com-

---

[1] J. T. Ford has drawn attention to this fact in "From Vatican I to the Present", *Journal of Ecumenical Studies*, 8 (1971), pp. 768–91 (781).

[2] O. Rousseau *et al.*, *L'Infaillibilité de l'Eglise* (Chèvetogne, 1962).

[3] B. Reynders, "Premières réactions de l'Eglise devant les falsifications du dépôt apostolique; Saint Irénée", *ibid.*, pp. 27–52.

[4] B.-D. Dupuy, "Le magistère de l'Eglise; service de la parole", *ibid.*, pp. 53–97.

[5] J. M. Todd *et al.*, *Problèmes de l'Autorité* (Paris, 1962).

[6] Y. Congar, *L'Ecclésiologie du Haut Moyen-Age* (Paris, 1968).

[7] *Idem*, *L'Eglise de St Augustin à l'époque moderne* (Paris, 1970).

[8] K. F. Morrison, *Tradition and Authority in the Western Church*, 300–1140 (Princeton, 1969).

[9] P. de Vooght, "Esquisse d'une enquête sur le mot 'infaillibilité' durant la période scolastique", *L'Infaillibilité de l'Eglise, op. cit.*, pp. 99–146.

petent authority within the Church. Tierney,[10] however, has modified this view and, like de Vooght, has rejected the idea of earlier writers such as von Döllinger and even of recent polemicists such as Küng that the canonists and decretists were guilty of this. Despite all the falsifications practised to increase Rome's authority and all the attempts to hold the Church by juridical means to this tradition, neither the pope nor the Church's councils were ever declared to be definitive *regula fidei* before 1300, nor were they given any specific *clavis scientiae* which would render them incapable of making wrong decisions.

According to Tierney, the concept was first applied to the Church's office as a counterbalance to the canonists' principle of sovereignty—*par in parem non habet imperium*—which meant that popes were not bound to the predecessors' decrees. Peter Olivi (d. 1298), Tierney believes, was the first writer to call the pope *regula inerrabilis fidei*, because he was afraid that later popes might modify Nicholas III's bull *Exiit*, which favoured the Franciscan way of life, thus according the same degree of authority to Nicholas's decisions as to Scripture and the articles of faith. It is not certain, however, whether Olivi acknowledged a special *clavis scientiae* in the case of the pope—this was first explicitly recognized in the so-called "Appeal of Sachsenhausen" (1384).

It is, however, clear from this Franciscan question that the possibility of heretical papal pronouncements could not be excluded, the concept of infallibility being here an *a posteriori* qualification of official statements that had been accepted previously because of their evangelical character. It would seem that it was Guido Terrena (d. 1342) who first gave it an *a priori* qualification. It is also possible to find in Terrena's work the later distinctions between the subject and the object of this qualification.

Several recent articles throw light on questions concerning the further development of the concept of infallibility not answered by Tierney,[11] especially those concerning the arguments of those

[10] B. Tierney, *Origins of Papal Infallibility, 1150–1350* (Leiden, 1972); Tierney himself has provided a summary of his work in the *Journal of Ecumenical Studies*, 8 (1971), pp. 841–64.

[11] See, for example, F. X. Seibel, "Die Kirche als Lehrautorität nach dem 'Doctrina Antiquitatum Fidei Catholicae Ecclesiae' des Thomas

who oppose this development and the connection between this concept and the notion of "continuity" in the statements made by the Church's magisterium, when so many authors have pointed to a discontinuity.[12] Tierney's conclusions with regard to whether the concept can still be used are audacious and one wonders whether his view of the concept at the time of Vatican I is not wrong. One of his conclusions, however, is very interesting—namely that the intention or content of the concept has changed in the course of history. What was this intention at the time of Vatican I?

II. VATICAN I

The detailed factual accounts of the events of Vatican I by Aubert,[13] Palanque,[14] Conzemius,[15] Lill,[16] Kasper,[17] Congar[18] and others have to be supplemented by textual studies such as those

---

Waldensis (um 1372–1431)", *Carmelus*, 16 (1969), pp. 3–69; U. Horst, "Papst, Bischöfe und Konzil nach Antonin von Florenz", *Recherches de Théologie Ancienne et Médiévale*, 32 (1965), pp. 76–116; idem, "Kirche und Papst nach Dominikus Bañez", *Freiburger Zeitschrift für Philosophie und Theologie*, 18 (1971), pp. 213–54; A. Molnar, "Infaillibilité et indéfectibilité de l'Eglise", *Communio Viatorum*, 14 (1971), pp. 155–64.

[12] R. Manselli in E. Castelli *et al.*, *L'Infaillibilité, son aspect philosophique et théologique* (Paris, 1970), pp. 113–30; H. Zimmermann, *Papstabsetzungen des Mittelalters* (Graz, Vienna and Cologne, 1968); P. de Vooght, "Les dimensions réelles de l'infaillibilité papale", *L'Infaillibilité, op. cit.*, pp. 131–58.

[13] R. Aubert, *Vatican I (Histoire des conciles oecuméniques*, 12) (Paris, 1964); idem, *Le Pontificat de Pie IX (1846–1878* (Paris, 1952); idem, "L'Ecclésiologie au Concile du Vatican", *Le concile et les conciles* (Gembloux, 1960), pp. 245–84; idem, "Die ekklesiologische Geographie im 19. Jahrhundert", *Sentire Ecclesiam* (Freiburg i. Br., 1961), pp. 440–73.

[14] J.-R. Palanque, *Catholiques libéraux et Gallicans en France face au concile du Vatican 1867–1870* (Aix-en-Provence, 1962).

[15] V. Conzemius, *Konzil im Bannkreis der Autorität* (Stuttgart, 1970); idem, "Lord Acton and the First Vatican Council", *Journal of Ecclesiastical History*, 20 (1969), pp. 267–94.

[16] R. Lill, "Historische Voraussetzungen des Dogmas vom Universalepiskopat und von der Unfehlbarkeit des Papstes", *Stimmen der Zeit* (1970), pp. 289–303.

[17] W. Kasper, *Die Lehre von der Tradition in der Römischen Schule* (Freiburg, Basle and Vienna, 1962).

[18] Y. Congar, "L'Ecclésiologie de la Révolution Française au Concile du Vatican sous le signe de l'affirmation de l'autorité", *Recherches de Science Religieuse*, 34 (1960), pp. 77–114.

found in a special collection published to mark the centenary of the Council.[19] F. van der Horst has also written a useful commentary on Kleutgen's second schema *De Ecclesia*, which was not discussed at the Council.[20]

Very detailed studies have been written by U. Betti on the Constitution *Pastor Aeternus*[21] and by H. Pottmeyer on *Dei Filius*.[22] The centenary was also marked by the appearance of G. Thils' illuminating study on the scope of the fourth chapter of *Pastor Aeternus* and thus on the dogma of papal infallibility.[23] All these authors have made use of the preparatory material dating back to 1867–1869 which has only recently been made public. Both Betti and Thils have used textual analysis and external sources to define more precisely such essential concepts as *definire; irreformabilis; ex sese, non autem ex consensu ecclesiae; ex cathedra; ea infallibilitate pollere qua divinus redemptor ecclesiam suam . . . instructam esse voluit; doctrina de fide vel moribus ab universa ecclesia tenenda*, etc. Both have also tried to indicate the limitations and conditions imposed by Vatican I itself on the exercise of papal infallibility.

Thils gives a relative value to the concept of infallibility, preferring the earlier and more comprehensive term *veritas*. He also insists that the Church's teaching office functions together with the community of believers, which in turn has an essential *infallibilitas in credendo* and that all statements made by the magisterium and the pope are governed by biblical revelation. Thils claims that his criticisms are ultimately based on the *acta* of Vatican I.

However much light is thrown on the problem by all these authors, it is undeniable that it is this very process of interpretation, so brilliantly exemplified in recent essays by Rahner[24] and

[19] *De doctrina Concilii Vaticani* (Città Vaticana, 1969).
[20] F. van der Horst, *Das Schema über die Kirche auf dem I. Vatikanischen Konzil* (Paderborn, 1963).
[21] U. Betti, *La Costituzione dommatica "Pastor Aeternus" del Concilio Vaticano I* (Rome, 1961).
[22] H. Pottmeyer, *Der Glaube vor dem Anspruch der Wissenschaft* (Freiburg, 1968).
[23] G. Thils, *L'Infaillibilité Pontificale. Source-conditions-limites* (Gembloux, 1969).
[24] K. Rahner, "Zum Begriff der Unfehlbarkeit in der katholischen Theologie. Einige Bemerkungen anlässlich des 100-Jahr-Jubiläums des Unfehl-

Congar,[25] that has led them to the position where they can say that modern Catholic theologians claim to accept the dogma of infallibility, but are able to by-pass it by means of hermeneutics. Tierney, for instance, says openly that, although all infallible statements are certainly true, not every statement is certainly infallible and that all infallible pronouncements are unchangeable until it seems better to change them.[26]

Thils also deals insufficiently with the *suprema auctoritas* of the dogma, which is linked to ideas about primacy which can no longer, since Vatican II, be formulated precisely in that way.[27] Moreover, nineteenth-century neo-scholastic thinking permeated all the debates and documents of Vatican I, which was overshadowed by the desire to strengthen the central authoritative structures of the Church and this is an attitude which is nowadays inevitably criticized.[28] The underlying intention of the Council, Thils maintains, obscured the perhaps more important questions of the relationship between the authority of Scripture and statements made by the Church's magisterium, the changing nature of the language of faith and the part played by the community of believers. It is therefore hardly surprising that the question has arisen, a hundred years later, as to whether the concept of infallibility can still be used.

III. CAN THE CONCEPT OF INFALLIBILITY STILL BE USED?

This question, first raised, for example, by H. Küng in his *Structures of the Church* and again in *The Church*, has become more and more pressing in recent years. An episcopal voice was

---

barkeitsdogmas vom 18. Juli 1870", *Stimmen der Zeit*, 186 (1970), pp. 18–31.

[25] Y. Congar, "Infaillibilité et Indéfectibilité", *Revue des Sciences Philosophiques et Théologiques*, 54 (1970), pp. 601–13; this essay is included in the author's *Ministères et Communion Ecclésiale* (Paris, 1971), pp. 141–57.

[26] Tierney, *op. cit.*, pp. 4–5.

[27] These questions are discussed by Thils in another work: *La Primauté pontificale. La doctrine de Vatican I. Les voies d'une révision* (Gembloux, 1972). A summary of this work will be found in the *Revue Théologique de Louvain*, 3 (1972), pp. 22–39.

[28] See the special number of *Tegenspraak*, 6 (18 July 1970), devoted to "a hundred years of infallibility".

raised in the debate when F. Simons' *Infallibility and the Evidence,* a book which is otherwise of little importance because of its outdated theological and philosophical framework, was published.[29]

Objections to the concept of infallibility have been made both on scriptural and hermeneutical grounds, which have led to a different concept of truth, and on the basis of a recognition that historical changes have taken place in man's experience of authority and his expression of faith.

At Rome University in 1970, the concept was discussed from the points of view of philosophy, theology, prayer, dogma, jurisdiction, history, and so on,[30] and the difficulty of distinguishing its function in these different spheres became apparent. These various aspects of infallibility together form the *charisma veritatis* of the Church's teaching office and this constitutes a *clavis scientiae,* a source of truth and knowledge. This mystification of the concept seems to verify itself[31] but inevitably conflicts with the biblical and theological understanding of truth of, for example, Rahner, Marlé, Tilliette and Pattaro and is the result of what Vergote calls a "pathology of infallibility" which occurs in many forms of religion. It is not in any sense in accordance with the medieval concept (Manselli) and is not favoured by Protestant theologians (Ulianich, Leuba).

From the ecumenical point of view, one conclusion that has been reached is that the concept should give way to a more biblical concept of truth,[32] whereas the Eastern Christians have called for more emphasis to be placed on the *consensus* of the Church and the *receptio* of the Church's statements by the community of believers. The alternative concept of "indefectibility"

[29] F. Simons, *Infallibility and the Evidence* (Springfield, 1968).

[30] E. Castelli *et al., L'Infaillibilité. Son aspect philosophique et théologique* (Paris, 1970).

[31] Among those opposed to this view are E. Nemesszeghy, "Infallibility and Logic", *The Heythrop Journal,* 9 (1968), pp. 179–83; K. Rahner, "Zu Begriff der Unfehlbarkeit", *Stimmen der Zeit,* 186 (1970), pp. 18–31; R. Panikkar, "Le sujet de l'infaillibilité. Solipsisme et Vérification", *L'Infaillibilité, op. cit.,* pp. 423–45.

[32] C. Moeller, "Conclusion: Infaillibilité et Vérité", *L'Infaillibilité de l'Eglise, op. cit.,* pp. 223–55 (252–55).

has also been suggested by Old Catholic and Anglican authors.[33] This brings us to Hans Küng's "enquiry".

IV. THE DEBATE ABOUT KÜNG's "INFALLIBLE? AN ENQUIRY"

This polemical book[34] initiated a lively discussion and an application on the part of many Catholic theologians of their hermeneutical skill, until then insufficiently developed, to the concept itself and to the dogma of 1870. We shall consider briefly some of the published reactions to Küng's book[35] after first summarizing the contents of his "enquiry".

In the first two chapters, Küng analyses the views about the infallibility of the pope and the episcopate that have emerged from manuals of theology, the documents of Vatican I and II and the debate about *Humanae Vitae*. These amount, in the concrete, to a mathematical way of thinking about truth, a conviction that dogma develops homogeneously in the Church and an acceptance of the principle of historical continuity in the Church's official teaching. Küng believes that these attitudes can be traced back to neo-scholasticism.

In the third chapter, he rejects this neo-scholastic interpretation of the biblical promises concerning the Lord's faithfulness to his Church and the help of the Holy Spirit and suggests forcefully that the Church has no need to make *a priori* infallible statements. What is, in his opinion, urgently required is a new biblical understanding of the Church's teaching office.

This idea is elaborated in the fourth chapter to embrace a new

[33] See, for example, M. D. Goulder *et al.*, *Infallibility in the Church. An Anglican-Catholic Dialogue* (London, 1968); L. Swidler, "The Ecumenical Problem Today: Papal Infallibility", *Journal of Ecumenical Studies*, 8 (1971), pp. 751–67.

[34] H. Küng, *Infallible? An Enquiry* (London, 1971).

[35] For the debate between Rahner and Küng, see G. Baum *et al.*, *The Infallibility Debate* (New York, 1971); G. Dejaifve, "Un debat sur l'infaillibilité. La discussion entre K. Rahner et H. Küng", *Nouvelle Revue Théologique*, 103 (1971), pp. 583–601; J. Carey, "Infallibility Revisited", *Theology Today*, 28 (1972), pp. 426–38; A. Kolping, *Unfehlbar. Eine Antwort* (Frankfurt and Mainz, 1971). A number of reactions will also be found in K. Rahner *et al.*, *Zum Problem Unfehlbarkeit* (Quaestiones Disputatae, 54) (Freiburg, Basle and Vienna, 1971). W. Kasper has reviewed these reactions in his article "Zur Diskussion um das Problem der Unfehlbarkeit", *Stimmen der Zeit*, 188 (1971), pp. 363–76.

concept of truth which departs from that of infallibility and is based on the notion of "remaining in the truth" and on a full acceptance of the part played by theologians and all believers within the Church's teaching office. Küng also discusses critically the Protestant principle of *sola Scriptura* and the Eastern Orthodox understanding of tradition in this context and points to the ecumenical perspectives that would be opened up by a different Catholic insight into the true nature of the ministry of Peter in the Church.

Certain national conferences of bishops reacted quickly to Küng's "enquiry"[36] and an investigation was set in motion by the Vatican.[37] The first interchanges between Küng and Rahner and Küng and Lehmann were rather acrimonious and often emotional, but very soon a number of convergences began to emerge.[38] Küng's use of the polemical style was criticized as

[36] See the declaration made by the conference of German bishops in *Herder Korrespondenz*, 25 (1971), pp. 156, 190; see also A. Antweiler's commentary on this declaration, "Fragen zur Erklärung der Deutschen Bischofskonferenz zum Buch Prof. Dr. Hans Küng, 'Unfehlbar? Eine Anfrage'", *Freiburger Zeitschrift für Philosophie und Theologie*, 18 (1971), pp. 499–511; Declaration of the Theological Commission of the Conference of French bishops, *Documentation catholique*, 68 (1971), 1583, 4 April 1971, p. 336; Declaration of the Commission for Teaching and Catechesis of the Italian bishops, *Documentation Catholique*, 68 (1971), 1581, 7 March 1971, p. 246; Declaration of Mgr Weber, Bishop of Strasbourg, *Documentation catholique*, 68 (1971), 1587, 6 June 1971, pp. 532–8.

[37] Küng's letter with a provisional answer to Mgr Seper in *Archief der Kerken*, 2 (1972), pp. 334–43.

[38] For the sake of convenience, I have grouped the reactions together under headings and have referred to the authors' names and to the page numbers of the articles listed below in alphabetical order. First of all, however, a number of reactions will be found in K. Rahner et al., *Zum Problem Unfehlbarkeit, op. cit.*, and in the debate between Küng and Rahner in *Stimmen der Zeit*, 186 (1970), pp. 361–77 (Rahner); 187 (1971), pp. 43–64, 105–22 (Küng); 187 (1971), pp. 145–60 (Rahner). See also G. Baum, "Truth in the Church. Küng, Rahner and Beyond", *The Ecumenist*, 9 (1971), pp. 33–48; W. Breuning and H. Schauf, "Unfehlbar?", *Theologische Revue*, 67 (1971), pp. 162–74; J. Carey, "Infallibility Revisited", *Theology Today*, 28 (1972), pp. 426–38; A. C. Cochrane, "The Promise of God and Ecclesiastical Propositions", *Journal of Ecumenical Studies*, 8 (1971), pp. 872–6; Y. Congar, "Infaillibilité et Indéfectibilité", addendum, *Revue des Sciences Philosophiques et Théologiques*, 54 (1970), pp. 614–18; G. Dejaifve, "Un debat sur l'infaillibilité. La discussion entre K. Rahner et H. Küng, *Nouvelle Revue Théologique*, 103 (1971), pp. 583–601; E. Jüngel, "Irren ist menschlich. Zur Kontroverse um Hans Küngs

aggressive, demagogic (Lehmann, p. 349), unscientific and even pseudo-scientific (Mühlen, p. 233), embracing too many subjects at the same time (Dejaifve, p. 600), leading to ambivalence (Ratzinger) and methodically lacking in purity (Lehmann, p. 347). Both Rahner and Ratzinger accused Küng of premature publication, resulting, according to Ratzinger, Brandmüller and Mühlen, in a lack of historical reliability in his arguments.

A second and more important convergence of opinion has been an almost universal agreement with Küng's rejection of the concept of "infallibility" in its almost all-embracing nineteenth-century interpretation, with his plea for a biblical concept of truth, for recognition of the "indefectibility" of the whole community of believers and of the inadequacy and changeable quality of the Church's formulation of faith and finally with his demand for dialogue and communication on the part of the Church's teaching office.

There is also a great deal of convergence concerning the objections to Küng's book. Firstly, many authors have objected to his raising of *Humanae Vitae* to the level of an infallible pronouncement on the part of the pope and the "Roman theologians". Secondly, Küng's interpretation of Vatican I has been criticized. It was never intended that the qualification "infallible" should be applied to *a priori* statements. According to Congar

---

Buch 'Unfehlbar? Eine Anfrage' ", *Evangelische Kommentare*, 4 (1971), pp. 75-80; W. Kasper, "Zur Diskussion um das Problem der Unfehlbarkeit", *Stimmen der Zeit*, 188 (1971), pp. 363-76; H. Küng, "L'Eglise selon l'Evangile. Réponse à Yves Congar", *Revue des Sciences Philosophiques et Théologiques*, 55 (1971), pp. 193-230; K. Lehmann, "Hans Küng auf Kollisionskurs? Eine Herausforderung zur Diskussion", *Publik*, 11 September 1970; *idem*, "Die Not des Widerspruchs", *Publik*, 29 January 1971; G. Lindbeck, "Hans Küng's 'Infallible' An Enquiry' ", *America*, 124 (1971/16), pp. 427-33; M. Löhrer, "Bemerkungen zu Hans Küng: 'Unfehlbar? Eine Anfrage' ", *Diakonia der Seelsorger*, 2 (1971), pp. 60-8; M. Sommer, "Kommunikation und Narzismus. Der Wahrheitsbegriff in der Kontroverse zwischen K. Rahner und H. Küng", *Trierer Theologische Zeitschrift*, 81 (1972), pp. 40-9; H. Stirnimann, " 'Bleiben in der Wahrheit' im Bereich der Sprache", *Freiburger Zeitschrift für Philosophie und Theologie*, 18 (1971), pp. 475-98; G. Thils, " 'Unfehlbar' de Hans Küng", *Revue Théologique de Louvain*, 2 (1971), pp. 88-96; J. P. Torrel, "A propos de l'infaillibilité pontificale", *Revue Thomiste*, 79 (1971), pp. 641-9; J. Visser, "Uberlegungen zu Hans Küngs Buch 'Unfehlbar' ", *Internationale Kirchliche Zeitschrift* (1971), pp. 272-87.

(p. 614), Fries (p. 222), Jüngel (p. 78), Kasper (p. 368), Lehmann (p. 364), Sartori (p. 91) and Scheffczyk (p. 162), the intention of Vatican I was to qualify persons and authoritative bodies as infallible—statements can only be called truthful, because there is nothing higher than the truth.

In this context, many objections—the third group—are concerned with Küng's concept of truth and many authors have concentrated on one sentence taken, moreover, from its context, namely that "every proposition can be both true and false". Sartori (p. 82), Scheffczyk (p. 159), Semmelroth (pp. 202–4), Lindbeck (p. 431) and Lehmann (p. 355) maintain that this marks a radical departure from traditional epistemological thought, whereas Rahner (pp. 369–72) believes that it leads to scepticism and Ratzinger (p. 115), Scheffczyk (p. 160) and Lehmann (p. 354) think that, because it excludes all criteria for the truth of statements, it is bound to lead to a totalitarian concept of truth.

Fourthly, Küng is accused of having a conceptualistic view of dogma as well as of truth, of concentrating too much on the truth of statements and too little on the underlying existential truth (Rahner, pp. 371–2) and of being too little aware of the "symbolic function" of dogma (Baum, Lindbeck), which is part of a communal process directed towards *consensus* and *communio* (Mühlen, pp. 252–7). God's promises, Cochrane insists (p. 875), cannot be dissociated from concrete assertions.

Fifthly, and most important of all, Küng's hermeneutical method is a stumbling-block for many of his critics. Rahner maintains that his thinking is not "immanent in the system" and Küng is also criticized for his too rigid adherence to the principle of *sola Scriptura* (Congar, p. 614, Semmelroth, p. 210, Knauer, p. 284) and for his neglect of "coherent explicitation" (Rahner, Sartori), thus leading to an abandonment of the Catholic tradition in interpretation (Rahner, Congar, Lehmann, Sartori, Thils, Ratzinger, Semmelroth).

Sixthly, and finally, Küng is accused of underestimating the importance of an authoritative teaching office in the Church (Congar, p. 614) and of making too sharp a division between that office and the function of theology (Ratzinger, p. 107).

It is not easy to assess the extent to which these objections can be applied to Küng's real intentions. He has in the main tried simply to clear up misunderstandings in most of his replies to his critics and, in his book, he often tones down challenging attitudes in later passages. Of all these authors, Kasper, Stirnimann, Baum and Lindbeck have understood perhaps most clearly that Küng's "enquiry" must not be taken as a definitive argument. Kasper has suggested that the whole problem should be further investigated from the point of departure that Christian truth is a "truth of testimony" and Stirnimann would like to replace the concept of infallibility by that of a *charisma veritatis*. Both are aware that the crux of the problem is the "historical" continuity of the event of faith and that a "homologous understanding of faith", which is, in other words, an assurance that the faith of the community of believers today is in accordance with God's intentions in Jesus Christ, is needed to safeguard this continuity. It is the Church's teaching office or rather its ministerial functions which guarantee this continuity, thus making it possible to speak of what Fries calls the "ultimate binding force" of the Church's proclamation of faith and dogma, so long as these ministerial functions are not dissociated from the faith of the whole community.

V. Conclusion

The ideas of continuity, reliability and certainty have always been central to the concept of infallibility, but there have been different emphases at different periods in the history of the Church, varying from the biblical "remaining in the truth" to the juridical extreme of an obligation to accept certain truths of faith. This historically based interpretation will undoubtedly not only throw a clearer light on the whole problem, but will also lead to a renewal of faith, especially if it is carried out by theologians of different Christian traditions.

Translated by David Smith

Hans Küng

A Short Balance-Sheet of the Debate on Infallibility

AS THE author of the book *Infallible? An Enquiry*, I have always freely admitted that I am not infallible. It surprises me that I have not been found guilty of more errors than confusing three ecumenical patriarchs in different centuries in such a complex book, in which I had to define my attitude with regard to so many questions at the same time. May I recall the motto of St Augustine which prefaced the book: "Let me ask of my reader ... wherever he recognizes me to be in error, there to call me back".

I. THE BACKGROUND TO THE BOOK

My "enquiry" into infallibility gave rise to the greatest debate among Catholic theologians that has taken place since Vatican II. The debate has extended far beyond the frontiers of theology and a balance-sheet is urgently required. The many criticisms of my book merit a detailed reply and this will be published this year, together with contributions by fifteen other theologians, a full documentation containing the correspondence with the Congregation of Faith and a bibliography.[1] In this book will be found full arguments and evidence for what is dealt with so briefly here—what has emerged from the debate on infallibility so deliberately unleashed after twelve years of preparation.

Ever since this preparation began with the publication of the

[1] *Fehlbar? Eine Bilanz* (Zürich, Einsiedeln and Cologne, 1973).

129

German original of my book *Justification* (*Rechtfertigung*) in 1957, I have again and again asked the question implicit in the very historicity of all dogmas, that is, their possible fallibility. I asked it very clearly in my *Structures of the Church* (1965), but it was ignored. It is precisely because of this long period of preparation that I chose to write my "enquiry" in a different style. The more gentle notes of my previous works had not aroused those in responsible positions in the Church, so I had to sound the alarm and they woke up suddenly and complained loudly. What did they complain about? The failure of leadership in the Church since Vatican II? The old and new forms of Roman imperialism? The enormous loss of credibility in the Church? The tens of thousands of priests who have given up their ministry because of the law of celibacy and the established structure of the Church or the crisis among the younger generation that has reached catastrophic proportions? The great suffering caused by wrong decisions concerning mixed marriages, the regulation of births, the appointment of bishops, celibacy and many other matters, in which the ordinary people have no say at all?

No, their complaints have been about the outspoken language of my book. There are cases, and this is one of them, where it is expedient to engage in polemics. The replies to my fair polemics have been polemical enough in themselves and I do not accept that serious polemics are necessarily unscientific. In other words, it is desirable to engage in polemics where it is expedient to do so.

In 1970, after the publication of my *The Theologian and the Church* in 1965, *Truthfulness* in 1968 and *The Church* in 1969, I came back to the old question and concluded that the time had come (1) to strip the Church's teaching office of the mythology and the false ideology that surrounded it and to free the Church from the dishonesty and the pretensions that have for so long characterized Vatican theology and administration; (2) to draw certain conclusions from the initiatives of Vatican II, at which no infallible definitions were made and a positive proclamation of Christian teaching was preferred to the traditional dogmatism of the Roman Church; (3) to make a loyal protest against the doctrinaire leadership in the post-conciliar Church, which has, in many ways—the regulation of births, mixed marriage, celibacy, the election of bishops, the Dutch Church, and so on—

resulted in human suffering; (4) to work for a solution to the four hundred and fifty-year-old problem of reunion between the churches in the West; (5) to consider once again the historical aspect of truth in the Church and to try once again to further Catholic renewal and to facilitate a break-through of the structure of the Church which is in so many ways contradictory to the Christian message.

II. RESULTS

1. My Catholicity can only be called into question if no distinction is made between authentic Catholicity in time and space as defined in *The Church* and the Roman Catholicism of the Church especially since the eleventh century. The juridicalism, imperialism, triumphalism and absolutism of this Roman system was sharply criticized during Vatican II and bishops, theologians and lay people have continued to criticize these characteristics of the Church ever since the Council as the main reason for the schism with the Eastern churches and the Protestant Reformation in the West.

2. My "enquiry" has been fully justified because no one has yet been able to raise any really convincing objections to my interpretation of the painful "infallibility" texts of Vatican I and II. The equally painful question about the "infallibility" of the teaching represented by *Humanae Vitae*—which only formed an opening to the book and was not central to my argument—proved to be a very suitable catalyst and was, significantly enough, supported even by "Roman" theologians when they found themselves unable to say anything constructive about the infallibility of the "ordinary" teaching office of the world episcopate.

3. The Catholic basis common to all participants in the debate is apparent from the fundamental agreement between myself and even my sharpest opponents. This is clear in three important ways.

(a) It was universally admitted with unexpected frankness that the Church's teaching office could be fallible and had in fact often erred.

(b) Even conservative theologians often regard the concept of infallibility as susceptible to misunderstanding and even as largely unintelligible today. If the infallibility of the pope had not already been defined, it would hardly be possible to define it now, as the social and historical conditions for such a definition would be lacking. The exaggerations and abuses of this dogma which have occurred in the hundred years since its definition and which, in my view, have their basis in the definition itself, are, of course, a frequent cause of complaint.

(c) Again, even conservative theologians regard the Church's remaining in the truth as more important than the infallibility of certain definitions. Therefore, since any errors on the part of the Church's teaching office cannot, at least in general, be disputed, at least fundamental and general consent is given to my positive argument, namely that the Church is maintained, despite all errors, in the truth of the Gospel.

4. Are there perhaps pronouncements, definitions, dogmas or propositions which are not only true (this is not disputed), but also infallibly true, since certain office-bearers are unable, because of the special help they receive from the Holy Spirit, to err in a given situation? It was precisely to this that the question mark in the title of my book *Infallible?* pointed. Yet there is general agreement that, in the whole of the debate so far, including the special seminar on infallibility held at Tübingen and attended by members of different schools at the university, not one theologian has been able to produce any proof of the possibility that the Holy Spirit guarantees the infallibility of certain pronouncements. Even the Congregation of Faith has not answered this question, which I have asked again and again in the correspondence.

5. Several other questions require further discussion (and this will in fact be found in the book to be published this year).

(a) What is the situation with regard to the dialectic of truth and error?

(b) How does a proposition that, according to its verbal formulation, that is in the abstract, can be true and false, become a true proposition in a given situation, that is, in the concrete?

(c) How can a proposition persist in history?

(d) How can a proposition about faith be both conditioned by its situation and at the same time binding?

6. Since the appearance of my book, my position has been unexpectedly confirmed from the Catholic side.

(a) The authentic but fallible authority of Peter and the question of Petrine succession has been further developed in recent exegetical investigations. However important Peter may have been to the Church in the post-apostolic period as a symbolic figure, there is little support in the New Testament for his infallibility—both positive and negative characteristics are to be found in all the biblical evidence. This applies *a fortiori* to any question of infallibility in the case of the bishop of Rome. What is more, the canonists of the Middle Ages never used, as evidence for papal infallibility, Luke 22. 32, which contains a promise to Peter not of inerrancy, but that he would preserve his faith to the end. The medieval canonists did not, moreover, apply this promise to the bishop of Rome, but to the whole Church.

(b) At the same time, recent studies in the development of dogma have also shown that, according to Athanasius and the early tradition of the Church, the authority of ecumenical councils is not based simply on their "ecumenical" character or on their definition of infallibly true propositions with the help of the Holy Spirit. On the contrary, their authority is derived from the witness they bear to Scripture and to the apostolic faith. In other words, they are authoritative in so far as they authentically and credibly proclaim the Gospel.

(c) Finally—and this has been perhaps the most surprising fact to emerge during the debate—recent historical research has revealed that the doctrine of papal infallibility did not develop slowly, but that it was quite a sudden creation at the end of the thirteenth century by Peter Olivi, a Franciscan theologian who was accused of heresy. It was not the classical medieval theologians and canonists or even the theologians of the Counter-Reformation who were ultimately responsible for the 1970 definition of infallibility, but rather the secular political and rationalist thinkers of the Counter-Reformation, de Lamennais and above all de Maistre. The medieval canonists—ecclesiology was at that time within their province—taught not that the faith of the Church was preserved by an infallible head, but that, however much the head of the Church might err from the truth, God would preserve the whole Church from error. This, of course, is completely in line with what I said in my book.

The result of these recent exegetical, dogmatic and historical studies is simply that my whole argument is even more in accordance with the great Catholic tradition than I originally believed.

III. The Possible Consensus of the Future

In the light of the debate that has so far taken place on the subject of infallibility, it would seem that it should be possible to reach a further consensus of opinion. In other words, an even more positive definition of how the Church can remain in the truth even without any infallible pronouncements is now a distinct possibility. This idea is more fully developed in the book about the debate that is to appear this year, but, in the meantime, a few brief notes will be of interest.

The indefectibility of the Church as the whole community of believers is in itself a truth of faith. This statement can be justified not merely by referring to a few classical texts, but by appealing to the whole Christian message, which finds faith as God's word addressed to man and which founds a community of believers. The Church is maintained in the truth wherever Jesus himself remains the truth for the individual or for a community and wherever man follows in his footsteps. This remaining in the truth is more a matter of orthopraxis than of orthodoxy. It is more a matter of individuals and of individual communities than of institutions. Truth is, after all, life lived in the fullness of the good news brought in Jesus Christ. This remaining in the truth is revealed—whenever it is not visible, as it often is not, in the hierarchy or in the teaching of the established Church—in the lived faith of the ordinary people, both inside the Church and outside it. The offices of the Church do not constitute truth in the Church. They have to serve truth in the Church and people in the Church.

The result of this is that the Church continues to live even in the case of serious error in faith or morals and that the Church must learn again and again how to live with errors. Errors are serious, but they do not threaten the life of the Church. The Church's criterion for truth in the Church is the Christian message as found in the New Testament and ultimately in Jesus Christ himself. This Christian message can be interpreted critically within the Christian community and the tradition of the Church. The Christian does not, in other words, ultimately believe in dogmas, statements or propositions, nor does he believe even in the Bible or in the Church. He believes in God himself and in Jesus Christ in whom God is revealed. His faith is certainly to some extent dependent on statements or propositions whenever he has to confess it, but it cannot be cancelled out by false statements or propositions.

In this way, the proclamation of the Christian message—both from day to day through the ordinary teaching office and in the extraordinary form of the teaching office—can be maintained in spite of individual errors, and bishops and the pope as well as councils can "function" and carry out their task even if they cannot define infallibly in cases of doubt who is right. The conflicts that are always likely to occur in the Church can also be more easily endured in this way.

A fallible teaching office must be accepted as providing an opportunity for the Church of the future to deal more easily with its errors. It may also be possible for a fallible Church to recover its earlier freedom and thus for the truth of the Gospel to be heard again more freely and despite all errors. Again, it may mean that, since sin can also be a *felix culpa*, error may similarly be a *felix error*. The truth of the Gospel will, after all, perhaps be more powerfully experienced through the Church's errors. Possibly too, the history of the Church will come to be viewed much more realistically and the Church's remaining in the truth will be seen in a much more convincing light.

A consensus of opinion of the kind that I have outlined so briefly here would also have to be an ecumenical consensus, implying possible faith on the part of other Christians in the indefectibility of the Church. This would remove the most serious obstacle to Christian unity. Even more important, however, is that it would make the Christian message much more credible to men living in the modern world. This is ultimately the only worth-while reason for the continued practice of theology today.

One final comment in conclusion—the heated discussion that has been taking place has shown clearly that a question of the complexity of "infallibility" cannot be settled by a unilateral decision on the part of the Church's teaching office. It is ultimately no more and no less than a question of truth. I can always be convinced by reasons, but we have to wait for these.

Translated by David Smith

Biographical Notes

Josef Blank was born in Ludwigshafen (Germany) in 1926 and was ordained in 1951. He studied at the Universities of Tübingen, Munich and Würzburg. He has been professor of New Testament Exegesis and Biblical Theology at the University of Saarland (Saarbrücken) since 1969. Among his published works are: *Krisis* (1964), *Paulus und Jesus* (1968), *Schriftauslegung in Theorie und Praxis* (1969), *Das Evangelium als Garantie der Freiheit* (1970), *Weiss Jesus mehr vom Menschen?* (1971), *Der Mensch am Ende der Moral* (1971), *Jesus von Nazareth, Geschichte und Relevanz* (1972). He has also contributed to many reviews and encyclopedias.

Yves Congar, o.p., was born in Sedan in 1904. He joined the Dominican Order in 1925 and was ordained in 1930. He teaches at the Faculty of Theology of the Saulchoir and is a member of the International Commission of Theologians. Among his numerous published works are: *La Tradition et les traditions*, 2 vols. (1960, 1963), *L'ecclésiologie du haut moyen âge* (1968), *L'Eglise de saint Augustin à l'époque moderne (Histoire des Dogmes III/3)* (1970), *Une, sainte, catholique et apostolique (Mysterium salutis)* (1970) and *Ministères et Communion ecclésiale* (1971).

Iring Fetscher was born in Marbach/Neckar (Germany) in 1922. He studied at the University of Tübingen and at the Sorbonne. Doctor of philosophy (1950) and a graduate in political sciences (1960), he is professor of political sciences at the Goethe University, Frankfurt. He was visiting professor at the Graduate Faculty of the New School for Social Research, New York (1968/69) and has lectured at Harvard University and in Japan, Italy, Spain and Finland. Among his published works are: *Hegels Lehre vom Menschen* (Stuttgart, 1970), *Von Marx zur Sowjetideologie* (Frankfurt, 1971[17]), *Rousseaus politische Philosophie* (Neuwied, 1968[2]) and *Karl Marx und der Marxismus* (Munich, 1967).

Canon Jean Giblet was born in Nivelles (Belgium) in 1918. Doctor of theology of Louvain (1949), licentiate in philosophy (1939) and in biblical sciences (1947), he is *professeur ordinaire* at the University of Louvain. Among his recent published works is *Recherches sur la théologie des ministères* (1969). He collaborated in the ecumenical translation of the Bible (*L'Evangile selon St Jean*, 1972).

ANTON HOUTEPEN was born in Etten-Leur (Netherlands) in 1940. He studied theology at Nijmegen and Heidelberg. He is an associate of the Pastoral Centre of the Diocese of Breda and of the Inter-University Institute for Ecumenical Questions at Utrecht.

HANS KÜNG was born in Sursee (Switzerland) in 1928. He is professor of dogmatic and ecumenical theology and director of the Institute of Ecumenical Research at the University of Tübingen. Among his published works are: *Die Kirche* (1967), *Wahrhaftigkeit* (1968), *Unfehlbar?* (1970), *Menschwerdung Gottes* (1970), *Wozu Priester?* (1971) and *Fehlbar?* (1973).

RENÉ LAURENTIN was born in Tours in 1917 and ordained in 1946. He studied at the Institut Catholique and at the Sorbonne, Paris. Docteur ès lettres, doctor of theology, he is professor of theology at the Catholic University of Angers and teaches in many foreign universities: in Canada (Montreal, Quebec), in the U.S.A. (Dayton) and in Latin America, etc. He was consultor to the Preparatory Theological Commission of Vatican II, then an official expert at the Council. He edits the religious chronicle of *Le Figaro* (Paris), is vice-president of the Société française d'études mariales and also carries on a pastoral ministry in the neighbourhood of Paris. Among his numerous published works, many on questions of Mariology and on Vatican II, are: *Développement et salut, Nouveaux ministères et fin du clergé, Réorientation de l'Eglise après le troisième Synode, Lourdes: Documents authentiques* (6 vols.), *La Vierge au Concile, Jésus et le Temple, Dieu est-il mort?, Crise et promesse de l'Eglise aux USA* and *Nouvelles dimensions de l'espérance*. He edits the Mariological chronicle of *La Revue des Sciences Philosophiques et Théologiques*.

PATRICK McGRATH was born in 1935. He studied theology at Maynooth and philosophy at Maynooth, Louvain and Oxford. Doctor of philosophy (Louvain, 1964), he is professor of philosophy at Maynooth. Among his published works is *The Nature of Moral Judgment* (London, 1967).

EDWARD SCHILLEBEECKX, O.P., was born in Antwerp in 1914 and was ordained in 1941. He studied at the Dominican Faculty of Theology of the Saulchoir, at the Ecole des Hautes Etudes and at the Sorbonne, Paris. Doctor of theology (1951) and master of theology (1959), he has been professor of dogmatic theology at the University of Nijmegen since 1958, and also a visiting professor at Harvard University. He is also editor-in-chief of *Tijdschrift voor Theologie*. Among his published works are: *Openbaring en theologie, God en mens, Wereld en Kerk, De zending van de Kerk, Geloofsverstaan: Interpretatie en kritiek* and *God, the Future of Man*.

GUSTAVE THILS was born in Brussels in 1909 and was ordained in 1931. He studied at the University of Louvain. Doctor and master of theology, he is professor of fundamental theology at the University of Louvain. Among his published works are: *Histoire doctrinale du mouvement oecuménique* (1963²), *Le Décret sur l'oecuménisme* (1966), *L'Eglise et les Eglises: Perspectives nouvelles en oecuménisme* (1967), *L'infaillibilité pontificale: Source, Conditions, Limites* (1969), *La primauté pontificale: La doctrine de Vatican I; Les voies d'une révision* (1972).